THE IMPACT
OF THE FRENCH REVOLUTION
ON ENGLISH LITERATURE

THE DOLPHIN

General Editor: Tim Caudery
Production Editor: Connie N. Relsted

19

THE IMPACT
OF THE FRENCH
REVOLUTION ON
ENGLISH LITERATURE

Edited by Anders Iversen

AARHUS UNIVERSITY PRESS

Editorial address:
The Dolphin
Department of English, Aarhus University
DK-8000 Aarhus C

Distribution:
Aarhus University Press
Building 170, Aarhus University
DK-8000 Aarhus C

ISBN 87 7288 369 3
ISSN 0106-4487
The Dolphin no. 19, autumn issue 1990

Subscription price for one year (two issues):
Europe 198 DKK, overseas US$ 38.00.
Single copy price (not including postage):
Europe 118 DKK, overseas US$ 19.65.
Back issues available - list sent on request.

Contents

'The Contrast 1793', by Thomas Rowlandson after Lord George Murray, 1 January 1793 (B.M. 8284). Reproduced by courtesy of the British Museum.

Preface

As the various acts of the French Revolution unfolded, contemporaries were well aware that they were watching a great drama, at once fearful and fascinating. In Britain, where the Revolution was followed closely, it gave rise to one of the liveliest debates in the history of the country. Later generations carried on the debate, and among historians and others it has never been closed. In a narrower sense the Revolution debate belongs to the first half of the 1790s, after which date the British government effectively quelled it and concentrated the resources and political energy of the nation on twenty years of war with Revolutionary and Napoleonic France.

This collection of essays takes up some aspects only of the British reaction to the Revolution. My own contribution, by way of introduction, deals with Burke's *Reflections on the Revolution*, the work which provoked Tom Paine to write his *Rights of Man*, which is here discussed by Mel Leiman.

There were writers in England who steered clear of the Revolution and the debate on it. One such was Jane Austen, whose elusive attitude to contemporary politics is traced with great care by John Dussinger. In contrast, the problem with Blake and Wordsworth is not their 'silence'. Both produced a succession of works in which they tried to come to terms with the Revolution. Ib Johansen conducts a wide-ranging tour through the Blakean universe, paying particular attention to the rhetoric of revolutionary (and counter-revolutionary) discourse, and Per Serritslev Petersen analyses Wordsworth's political and philosophical development in terms of *four* revolutions ('no more, no less!').

The second generation of Romantic poets, confronting a situation of political repression and reaction at home, might turn to the Revolution for inspiration, but the Revolution proper was past history, and France was under the rule of Napoleon and - after 1815 - of the restored Bourbon monarchy. Jørgen Erik Nielsen, finding very few references to the French Revolution in Byron's writings, argues that his political ideals and in particular his advocacy of liberty were primarily shaped by Whig attitudes and by what he had read about antiquity and America. Karsten Klejs Engelberg shows how Shelley, after his early support of various radical causes, turned away in frustration from practical politics, and - retaining his idealism - made the revolutionary spirit 'a permanent, necessary, and deeply individual state of mind', as best exemplified in *Prometheus Unbound*.

In the last article Knud Sørensen offers a stylistic study of Carlyle's *The French Revolution* and Dickens's *A Tale of Two Cities*. Carlyle's passionate involvement with the course of the Revolution (where he had 'the Bastille to take' a second time, and even a third time after John Stuart Mill accidentally set fire to the first volume of Carlyle's manuscript) is reflected in the subjective style with a plethora of mannerisms and a very extensive use of the historic or dramatic present. Dickens was a great admirer of Carlyle and relied heavily on his work on the Revolution for his own *Tale of Two Cities*. Knud Sørensen concludes that Carlyle's work was meant as a warning, and so was Dickens's: 'What happened in France might well happen in England.'

My thanks are due to Connie Relsted and Tim Caudery. Without their technical expertise and editorial efficiency this issue of *The Dolphin* would never have seen the light of day.

Anders Iversen

Burke and the Debate on the Revolution

Anders Iversen

1. Revolution

When an eighteenth-century Englishman talked about the Revolution, he usually meant the English Revolution, the so-called Glorious Revolution of 1688-89, the *coup d'état* which had sent James II packing and filled the throne ('being vacant') with William-and-Mary. The Great Rebellion was the term used to refer to the Civil War and the political and social upheaval of the two middle decades of the seventeenth century, a sequence of events which today will more often seem to merit the revolutionary label.

The word *revolution* has had a number of meanings, both positive and negative, from the orbital motion of planets and other heavenly bodies, or the rotation of the wheel of fortune, to fundamental (and often dramatic) changes in social and political conditions. In his *Reflections on the Revolution in France* Edmund Burke uses the word about the Glorious Revolution, also of course about the French Revolution, and at least once about the events of the 1640s and 1650s.[1]

The French *Revolution* was so called from the beginning, and has remained *the* Revolution. It was followed with great interest all over Europe, and with mixed feelings. In Britain many people welcomed it with enthusiasm. Wordsworth was one of them: 'Bliss was it in that dawn to be alive, But to be young was very Heaven!' He was one of the few Englishmen who had first-hand experience of the Revolution, and his changing attitude to it - from enthusiasm via disillusionment to despair - described a revolution in itself, as we can see from his record of the 'growth of a poet's mind' in *The Prelude*.

In Britain there had long been a campaign for political reform (extension of the franchise, redistribution of parliamentary seats, lifting of the disabilities of Catholics and Protestant dissenters). One of the leaders of the movement was Richard Price, a moral philosopher and a mathematician and also a prominent Dissenting preacher. Like many other Dissenters, Price greeted the French Revolution with great expectations. It would be an inspiration for British reformers and hold out a hope to all mankind.

Burke watched the goings-on in France with scepticism and anxiety from the start, but it was his reading (probably in January 1790) of a sermon by Richard Price that kindled his passion and made him train his formidable powers of analysis and argument on French revolutionaries and more particularly on their British supporters. Price's sermon ('A Discourse on the Love of our Country') had been delivered to the Society for Commemorating the Revolution in Great Britain, on November 4, 1789, the anniversary of the Revolution of 1688.

2. Burke's *Reflections*

The full title of Burke's work is: 'Reflections on the Revolution in France, and on the Proceedings in Certain Societies in London Relative to that Event. In a Letter intended to have been sent to a Gentleman in Paris.' The gentleman in question was one Chames-Jean-François de Pont, a young man who had written a letter to Burke asking for his opinion on the revolutionary proceedings in France. Burke wrote a reply and sent it to de Pont, perhaps early in January 1790. A prefatory note to *Reflections* informs us that Burke received another letter from his French correspondent, and this made him begin 'a second and more full discussion on the subject' (p. 84), again in the form of a letter.

Soon after, it would seem, Burke first read Richard Price's 'Discourse', which inflamed and inspired him to write his *Reflections*, published in November 1790. The double inspiration behind the work is reflected in its form and contents. Price remains the *bête noire*, and the British public may be said to be the immediate addressee, but formally the book is directed to a Frenchman and written also with a French audience in mind. Upon publication it was immediately translated into French.

The book deals with the first year of the French Revolution and its background, at fairly great length and - particularly in the last third - in some detail, but there is almost as much about the Revolution's reception in Britain and its potentially pernicious influence on British society. The bifocal quality of the book and a number of overlappings have made it inordinately long, and it is not at all clearly structured.

Burke himself realized that the letter form was not appropriate for such a long pamphlet: 'A different plan, he is sensible, might be more favourable to a commodious division and distribution of his matter' (Prefatory note, p. 84). But 'he found it difficult to change the form of address', and speaking directly to his French correspondent he says:

> Solicitous chiefly for the peace of my own country, but by no means unconcerned for your's, I wish to communicate more largely, what was at first intended only for your private satisfaction. I shall still keep your affairs in my eye, and continue to address myself to you. Indulging myself in the freedom of epistolary intercourse, I beg leave to throw out my thoughts, and express my feelings, just as they arise in my mind, with very little attention to formal method.
>
> (p. 92)

Burke did not find the time to recast his material into a more suitable mould. He was overworked and had to snatch (as he said, p. 376) the hours he gave to *Reflections* from his major occupation in those years: conducting the impeachment proceedings against Warren Hastings. The work, then, is not a systematic treatise, but despite its structural weaknesses it still appeals to the modern reader, for it discusses fundamental social and political problems with great penetration and insight, and it is written with passion and vigour. In many parts it is compulsively readable.

In the following years Burke published several other works on the French Revolution, but here I shall concentrate on *Reflections*.

3. Anti-revolutionary

Because of the connotations of the word counter-revolution it would be incorrect to call Burke a counter-revolutionary, but anti-revolutionary he certainly was, although he recognized that in certain extreme circumstances a revolution might be the only way out, as for example in England in 1688. Necessity knows no law, but the *ancien régime* of France was not, in Burke's view, a tyranny that could have made a revolution necessary and justifiable. He did not like the 'continual talk of resistance and revolution', and warned against 'the practice of making the extreme medicine of the constitution its daily bread' (p. 154). As for the National Assembly (created when the Estates-General, or rather the Third Estate, proclaimed itself the National Assembly), Burke considered it nothing but an unauthorized 'voluntary association of men' who had seized the power of the state (p. 275).

> [The National Assembly is] a power, which has derived its birth from no law and no necessity; but which on the contrary has had its origin in those vices and sinister practices by which the social union is often disturbed and sometimes destroyed. This assembly has hardly a year's prescription. We have their own word for it that they have made a revolution. To make a revolution is a measure which, *prima fronte*, requires an apology. To make a revolution is to subvert the ancient state of our country; and no common reasons are called for to justify so violent a proceeding.
>
> (p. 276)

Burke believed in the opposite of revolution - the slow accumulation of experience in individuals and - so to speak - in generations of men and their institutions. Men of experience knew that one should not rashly abolish that which had stood the test of time. It was always easy to destroy institutions and raze them to the ground, but it would be better to amend and reform: to repair the walls and build on the old foundations (see pp. 121 and 152). A true statesman will seek a *via media*:

> There is something else than the mere alternative of absolute destruction, or unreformed existence. ... I cannot conceive how any man can have brought himself to that pitch of presumption, to consider his country as nothing but *carte blanche*, upon which he may scribble whatever he pleases. A man full of warm speculative benevolence may wish his society otherwise constituted than he finds it; but a good patriot, and a true politician, always considers how he shall make the most of the existing materials of his country. A disposition to preserve, and an ability to improve, taken together, would be my standard of a statesman. Everything else is vulgar in the conception, perilous in the execution.
>
> (pp. 266-267)

If Burke's ideal - 'at once to preserve and to reform' - is to be achieved, it requires on the part of the politician a rare combination of qualities, such as 'a vigorous mind, steady persevering attention, various powers of comparison and combination' *and* patience, and if it is objected that such a mode of reforming might take up many years, his answer is: 'Without question it might; and it ought' (p. 280).

> Political arrangement, as it is a work for social ends, is to be only wrought by social means. There mind must conspire with mind. Time is required to produce that union of minds which alone can produce all the good we aim at. Our patience will achieve more than our force.
>
> (p. 281)

Burke's veneration for that which holds society together is based on religion and a gentlemanly ethos, and finds expression at a practical and legal level in his passionate defence of rights of property and prescription. In his reaction to the Enlightenment, which he regarded as a shallow philosophy, he even went to the length of defending, somewhat paradoxically, prejudices and superstitions for their social and moral value (see for example pp. 183 and 269). This attitude of his also made him tolerant of various institutional inequalities and absurdities. Thus he dismissed the campaign for parliamentary electoral reform as simply irrelevant, and even defended what was perhaps the most absurd single feature of the unreformed pre-1832 system, the grotesque over-representation of Cornwall, which with a total electorate of less than 1400 had 21 parliamentary boroughs and 44 MPs (including the two county representatives).

> When did you hear in Great Britain of any province suffering from the inequality of its representation; what district from having no representation at all? ... The very inequality of representation, which is so foolishly complained of, is perhaps the very thing which prevents us from thinking or acting as members for districts. Cornwall elects as many members as all Scotland. But is Cornwall better taken care of than Scotland?
>
> (pp. 303-304)

Moving beyond the narrow sphere of political engineering, Burke also seems to look at social inequalities and subordination with an indulgent eye. He refers to a 'true moral equality of mankind', but dwells more on 'that real inequality' which is irremovable (p. 124). The real inequality, both genetically and socially determined, is a condition which the underprivileged have to come to terms with.

> The body of the people must not find the principles of natural subordination by art rooted out of their minds. They must respect that property of which they cannot partake. They must labour to obtain what by labour can be obtained; and when they find, as they commonly do, the success disproportioned to the endeavour, they must be taught their consolation in the final proportions of eternal justice.
>
> (p. 372)

Those who should be blamed, the cruel oppressors, are those who try to deprive the poor of such consolation! If this sounds like the callous conventional wisdom of the eighteenth century (Whatever is, is right), it should be added that Burke was not uncritical of contemporary British society. As a prominent Member of Parliament, and in his many writings, he had criticized abuses and campaigned for the rights of his Irish compatriots and of the American colonists. He had been the prime mover in what resulted in the so-called Economical Reform (1782) curtailing the government's power to manipulate (or buy support in) Parliament, and he organized the impeachment proceedings against Warren Hastings.

Against the background of this liberal reformist record, *Reflections on the Revolution in France* came as an unpleasant surprise to many contemporaries used to considering Burke a reforming Whig. It is true that in this work the balance between conservative and reforming ideas had tipped in favour of conservatism, but it was a change of emphasis, not a *volte-face*. He was not against reforms, but he was against innovations whose extent and effect could not be calculated, just as he was against *liberty* in the abstract without due attention to *circumstances*.

> I flatter myself that I love a manly, moral, regulated liberty as well as [anybody] ... and perhaps I have given as good proofs of my attachment to that cause, in the whole course of my public conduct. ... But I cannot stand forward, and give praise or blame to any thing which relates to human actions, and human concerns, on a simple view of the object, as it stands stripped of every relation, in all the nakedness and solitude of metaphysical abstraction. Circumstances (which with some gentlemen pass for nothing) give in reality to every political principle its distinguishing colour, and discriminating effect. The circumstances are what render every civil and political scheme beneficial or noxious to mankind.
> . . .
> I must be tolerably sure, before I venture publicly to congratulate men upon a blessing, that they have really received one. ... I should therefore suspend my congratulations on the new liberty of France, until I was informed how it had been combined with government; with public force; with the discipline and obedience of armies; with the collection of an effective and well-distributed revenue; with morality and religion; with the solidity of property; with peace and order; with civil and social manners. All these (in their way) are good things too; and, without them, liberty is not a benefit whilst it lasts, and is not likely to continue long.
>
> (pp. 89-91)

4. The English Revolution

The Glorious Revolution, as the name suggests, has been celebrated by its victors and beneficiaries - the Whigs - and their historians, and the Whig interpretation remained influential in English historiography until the second third of the twentieth century. To mark the 250th anniversary of the Revolution, George Macaulay Trevelyan, the last great representative of the Whig school of history, published a book in 1938, in which he characterized the Revolution Settlement as being at once liberal and conservative. The only revolutionary act was the expulsion of James II, but 'otherwise the spirit of this strange Revolution was the opposite of revolutionary.' Its keynote was 'personal freedom under the law, both in religion and in politics. The most conservative of all revolutions in history was also the most liberal'.[2]

We find a very similar view of the events of 1688-89 expressed in Burke's *Reflections*. There was, in the person of William III, 'a small and a temporary deviation from the strict order of a regular hereditary succession' (p. 101), but otherwise there was no interference with 'the healthy habit of the British constitution', namely the hereditary succession of the crown (p. 109). Richard Price's claim that since 1688 the English king 'owes his crown to the *choice of his people*' (p. 96), only showed how seriously Price had misunderstood the Revolution Settlement. It was not intended as a break with the past, as an innovation. On the contrary, it was meant to defend and safeguard hereditary rights, and to make it possible to go on deriving 'all we possess as *an inheritance from our forefathers*' (p. 117).

> The people of England ... look upon the legal hereditary succession of their crown as among their rights, not as among their wrongs; as a benefit, not as a grievance; as a security for their liberty, not as a badge of servitude.
>
> (p. 111)

> ... from Magna Charta to the Declaration of Right [1689], it has been the uniform policy of our constitution to claim and assert our liberties, as an *entailed inheritance* derived to us from our forefathers, and to be transmitted to our posterity; as an estate specially belonging to the people of this kingdom without any reference whatever to any other more general or prior right. By this means our constitution preserves an unity in so great a diversity of its parts. We have an inheritable crown; an inheritable peerage; and a house of commons and a people inheriting privileges, franchises, and liberties, from a long line of ancestors.
>
> (p. 119)

5. The French Revolution

Burke throughout uses the English Revolution and the British constitution as a yardstick to measure the revolutionary goings-on in France and the new political and social realities. His main point is that the French Revolution was rash, superfluous and counter-productive in terms of its professed aims. It was only useful as a warning to other nations against what could happen when a government, losing its nerve and sense of direction, under popular pressure opened the floodgates to 'innovation'.

Burke's judgement on the Revolution was, in its turn, over-hasty and based on inadequate information on, and familiarity with, France. His *Reflections* astonished many contemporaries because the book came out at a time of relative calm, a lull after the early excesses of the Revolution. Other observers thought that the Revolution was about to take a more moderate course and would result in a constitutional (limited) monarchy, but Burke had been thoroughly upset by the eruption of mob violence, by the collapse of law and order, the confiscations of church property, etc. He may have exaggerated and over-reacted, but his instincts or extrapolations turned out to be uncannily prescient.

As early as 1790 Burke had foreseen what 'the terror of the bayonet, and the lamp-post' (for hangings) might lead to (p. 160), had seen with his mind's eye the gallows 'at the end of every visto', and had predicted the rise to power of 'some popular general', who will be 'the master ... of your king, the master of your assembly, the master of your whole republic' (p. 342). Burke laid the blame for the unlawfulness and general misery on the Enlightenment philosophy ('this new conquering empire of light and reason'):

> On the scheme of this barbarous philosophy, which is the offspring of cold hearts and muddy understandings, and which is as void of solid wisdom, as it is destitute of all taste and elegance, laws are to be supported only by their own terrors, and by the concern, which each individual may find in them, from his own private speculations, or can spare to them from his own private interests. In the groves of *their* academy, at the end of every visto, you see nothing but the gallows. Nothing is left which engages the affections on the part of the commonwealth. On the principles of this mechanic philosophy, our institutions can never be embodied, if I may use the expression, in persons; so as to create in us love, veneration, admiration, or attachment.
>
> (pp. 171-172)

Burke dwells at some length and with gory details on the October Days of 1789 when a Parisian mob and the National Guard marched to Versailles and forced the King and Queen to accompany them back to Paris, where the royal family were installed in the Tuileries ('now converted into a Bastile for kings' (p. 165)). Echoing a passage in Richard Price's sermon, Burke with bitter irony refers more than once to 'this famous triumph' from Versailles to Paris, but the most remarkable feature of the description is the ominous note on which it ends:

> The actual murder of the king and queen, and their child, was wanting to the other auspicious circumstances of this '*beautiful day*'. The actual murder of the bishops, though called for by so many holy ejaculations [Tous les évêques à la lanterne], was also wanting. A groupe of regicide and sacrilegious slaughter, was indeed

16

boldly sketched, but it was only sketched. It unhappily was left unfinished in this great history-piece of the massacre of innocents. What hardy pencil of a great master, from the school of the rights of men, will finish it, is to be seen hereafter.

(p. 166)

The above passage with its indignation and heavy irony is followed closely by one of the most notorious descriptions in Burke: the idealized picture of the French royal family and particularly the idolization of Queen Marie Antoinette, whom he had seen some sixteen years earlier while she was still the dauphiness. He recalls her, semi-divine, in a mixture of cosmic vision and sentimental idyll:

... surely never lighted on this orb, which she hardly seemed to touch, a more delightful vision. I saw her just above the horizon, decorating and cheering the elevated sphere she just began to move in, - glittering like the morning-star, full of life, and splendor, and joy.

(p. 169)

Such abrupt changes of tone might give the impression that Burke was mentally off balance or hysterical. At least his emotionalism and passion bespeak the intensity of his concern about the French challenge to all that he most firmly believed in.

As for writers and intellectuals without his own extensive political experience, he poured scorn on them as 'democratists', 'speculatists', 'professors of metaphysics', etc., and on Dr Price in particular: 'this *political* Preacher' (pp. 143-152). To illustrate what it was that more directly had provoked Burke, I shall quote in full the peroration of Price's 'Discourse on the Love of our Country', the sermon he delivered to the Revolution Society on November 4, 1789.

What an eventful period is this! I am thankful that I have lived to it; and I could almost say, *Lord, now lettest thou thy servant depart in peace, for mine eyes have seen thy salvation.* I have lived to see a diffusion of knowledge, which has undermined superstition and error - I have lived to see the rights of men better understood than ever; and nations panting for liberty, which seemed to have lost the idea of it. - I have lived to see THIRTY MILLIONS of people, indignant and resolute, spurning at slavery, and demanding liberty with an irresistible voice; their king led in triumph, and an arbitrary monarch surrendering himself to his subjects. - After sharing in the benefits of one Revolution, I have been spared to be a witness to two other Revolutions, both glorious. - And now, methinks, I see the ardour for liberty catching and spreading; a general amendment beginning in human affairs; the dominion of kings changed for the dominion of laws, and the dominion of priests giving way to the dominion of reason and conscience.

Be encouraged, all ye friends of freedom, and writers in its defence! The times are auspicious. Your labours have not been in vain. Behold kingdoms,

17

admonished by you, starting from sleep, breaking their fetters, and claiming justice from their oppressors! Behold, the light you have struck out, after setting AMERICA free, reflected to FRANCE, and there kindled into a blaze that lays despotism in ashes, and warms and illuminates EUROPE!

Tremble all ye oppressors of the world! Take warning all ye supporters of slavish governments, and slavish hierarchies! Call no more (absurdly and wickedly) REFORMATION, innovation. You cannot now hold the world in darkness. Struggle no longer against increasing light and liberality. Restore to mankind their rights; and consent to the correction of abuses, before they and you are destroyed together.[3]

Returning to the letter form for a few moments, Burke warns his French correspondent against believing that Price and his ilk 'represent the opinions and dispositions generally prevalent in England' (p. 181). Burke also finds it outrageous that the Revolution Society should have sent an address of support and congratulation to the French National Assembly (p. 159). Enthusiasts like Richard Price and Lord Stanhope (chairman of the Revolution Society) are dangerous, because they help to spread the revolutionary contagion in their own country, but Burke knows how to cut them down to size:

Because half a dozen grasshoppers under a fern make the field ring with their importunate chink, whilst thousands of great cattle, reposed beneath the shadow of the British oak, chew the cud and are silent, pray do not imagine, that those who make the noise are the only inhabitants of the field; that of course, they are many in number; or that, after all, they are other than the little shrivelled, meagre, hopping, though loud and troublesome insects of the hour.

(p. 181)

6. An Irish Spokesman for England

Burke distinguishes sharply 'the *real* rights of men' from what he calls the false claims of right. To the latter category belong 'the rights of men' of the *philosophes* and the French Revolution. These spurious rights are like an underground mine that will blow up 'all examples of antiquity, all precendents, charters and acts of Parliament'. Against these newfangled 'rights' there can be no prescription; 'against these no agreement is binding' (p. 148). We enter a less speculative, more concrete and practical world when we turn to the *real* rights of men, as Burke understands them.

If civil society be made for the advantage of man, all the advantages for which it is made become his right. It is an institution of beneficence; and law itself is only beneficence acting by a rule. Men have a right to live by that rule; they have a right to justice ... They have a right to the fruits of their industry; and to the means of making their industry fruitful. They have a right to the acquisitions of their

18

parents; to the nourishment and improvement of their offspring; to instruction in life, and to consolation in death.

(p. 149)

With his lawyer's mind Burke approaches the problems of society and government in an empirical, analytical way and shuns theoretical discussion of 'metaphysic rights' which would only exist in a vacuum, not in civil society.

> The [real] rights of men are in a sort of *middle*, incapable of definition, but not impossible to be discerned. The rights of men in governments are their advantages; and these are often in balances between differences of good; in compromises sometimes between good and evil, and sometimes between evil and evil. Political reason is a computing principle; adding, subtracting, multiplying, and dividing, morally and not metaphysically or mathematically, true moral denominations.

(p. 153)

The science of government, says Burke, is therefore a practical science, and like every other experimental science, it is not to be taught *a priori*. 'Nor is it a short experience that can instruct us in that practical science' (p. 152).

From here Burke proceeds to equate the theoretical school with France, the practical school with Britain, and in the comparison France comes out second best. He finds in the British 'national character' a 'sullen resistance to innovation' and a 'cold sluggishness', qualities which in this context turn out to be peculiar excellences in that they have prevented the British from being converted and seduced by Rousseau, Voltaire and Helvetius: '[We have not] subtilized ourselves into savages. ... Atheists are not our preachers; madmen are not our lawgivers' (pp. 181-182).

This is Burke at his most conservative, his most traditionalist. He even assumes a somewhat John Bullish character ('the simplicity of our national character, ... a sort of native plainness and directness of understanding' (p. 186)), a role that sits rather uneasily on him. This John Bull is 'a religious animal' before he is a political animal (p. 187). In his simple, plain and direct way he is an establishment figure: '[R]eligion is the basis of civil society, and the source of all good and all comfort' (p. 186), and religion is of course Establishment religion. Burke, the Irishman at least half of whose family was Catholic, puts it very firmly (as if he needed to convince himself): 'We are protestants, not from indifference but from zeal' (p. 187). And there is a similar firmness when he sums up the quintessential Britishness of his stance: 'We are resolved to keep an established church, an established monarchy, an established aristocracy, and an established democracy, each in the degree it exists, and in no greater' (p. 188).

19

Whatever is, is right!

Burke had come to London as an Irish outsider, a brilliantly gifted man of letters who made politics his career without ever attaining cabinet office. Economically he could never feel secure, and socially he was never fully accepted by the aristocrats (the Rockingham Whigs) whose spokesman and pamphleteer he was. It is little wonder that his voice sometimes sounded both strained and strident. It is, one would think, a case of being *plus royaliste que le roi*. We have already seen how his defence of the institution of monarchy could turn into fulsome adulation, and there are other examples in the writings on the French Revolution from his declining years, when he was becoming more isolated politically.

7. The Little Platoon

Re-reading Burke today - 200 years after his book was first published - is an interesting experience, after the collapse of a dozen regimes that went back, directly or indirectly, to revolutions in the first two decades of this century, and after the disintegration of much of the ideology which they claimed to be based on. On the whole he has stood up well. His economic analysis of the French Revolution is remarkably perceptive, but his greatest appeal today would probably be his warnings against 'theorists' and 'metaphysicians' willing to sacrifice human beings by the million on the altar of their theories or ideologies, and also - in a period of re-emerging nationalism - his feel for social cohesion and his comprehensive view of human nature, including that second nature which is the product of life in society (see pp. 299-300).

When he talks about society in general terms, he can invest the social contract with grandiosity and at the same time immediacy: 'Society is indeed a contract. ... It is a partnership in all science; a partnership in all art; a partnership in every virtue, and in all perfection. ... a partnership not only between those who are living, but between those who are living, those who are dead, and those who are to be born' (pp. 194-195).

Burke's starting-point is not a blueprint of society, not liberty in the abstract, but a particular issue or certain 'circumstances', something concrete. Society must be considered as an organism, and from the bottom up.

> To be attached to the subdivision, to love the little platoon we belong to in society, is the first principle (the germ as it were) of public affections. It is the first link in the series by which we proceed towards a love to our country and to mankind.
> (p. 135)

We begin our public affections in our families. No cold relation is a zealous citizen. We pass on to our neighbourhoods, and our habitual provincial connections. These are inns and resting-places. ... The love to the whole is not extinguished by this subordinate partiality. Perhaps it is a sort of elemental training to those higher and more large regards, by which alone men come to be affected, as with their own concern, in the prosperity of a kingdom so extensive as that of France.

(p. 315)

8. Equipoise

At the end of his *Reflections*, after the extended examination and evaluation of the political institutions of the French Revolution (pp. 284 ff), Burke turns to the British constitution to recommend it to the French as a better model than any they have themselves devised. Like Blackstone, Burke valued it for its happy balance and its long history.

I think our happy situation owing to our constitution; but owing to the whole of it, and not to any part singly; owing in a great measure to what we have left standing in our several reviews and reformations, as well as to what we have altered or super-added. ... I would not exclude alteration neither; but even when I changed, it should be to preserve. I should be led to my remedy by a great grievance. In what I did, I should follow the example of our ancestors. I would make the reparation as nearly as possible in the style of the building.

(p. 375)

In the last paragraph of *Reflections* Burke looks back, sketching his own political portrait, as it were: a man 'almost the whole of whose public exertion has been a struggle for the liberty of others', and - changing the metaphor - a man wanting to steer a middle course and on an even keel: and so 'when the equipoise of the vessel in which he sails, may be endangered by overloading it upon one side, [he] is desirous of carrying the small weight of his reasons to that which may preserve its equipoise' (pp. 376-377).

9. Epilogue

Burke has often been called the father of modern conservatism. That is a dubious description, if it leads us to approach him in modern party-political terms. To Burke there was no insuperable opposition between conservative and reforming. One could be at once liberal and conservative, as Burke was. This was recognized by the young Harold Laski, who paid a remarkable tribute to his work. He called Burke 'the permanent manual of political wisdom', and said that no English statesman had ever 'more firmly moved amid a mass of details to the principle they involve'. In that 'middle ground between the facts and speculation his supremacy is unapproached.'[4]

The French Revolution cannot be summed up in a paragraph, and no final judgement will ever be passed on it. Nevertheless I shall quote the concluding lines of William Doyle's recent history of the Revolution, for they bring together a number of the themes I have touched on above.[5]

> [The French Revolution] transformed men's outlook. The writers of the Enlightenment, so revered by the intelligentsia who made the Revolution, had always believed it could be done if men dared to seize control of their own destiny. The men of 1789 did so, in a rare moment of courage, altruism, and idealism which took away the breath of educated Europe. What they failed to see, as their inspirers had not foreseen, was that reason and good intentions were not enough by themselves to transform the lot of their fellow men. Mistakes would be made when the accumulated experience of generations was pushed aside as so much routine, prejudice, fanaticism, and superstition. The generation forced to live through the upheavals of the next twenty-six years paid the price. Already by 1802 a million French citizens lay dead; a million more would perish under Napoleon, and untold more abroad. How many millions more still had their lives ruined? Inspiring and ennobling, the prospect of the French Revolution is also moving and appalling: in every sense a tragedy.

Notes

1. All references to Edmund Burke's *Reflections on the Revolution in France* are to the Pelican edition, ed. Conor Cruise O'Brien, Harmondsworth, Middlesex: Penguin Books, published in Pelican edition 1968, reprinted 1973. Page references, e.g. (p. 169), are given in brackets in the text immediately following the quotation. Misprints apart, Burke's text has a number of irregular or idiosyncratic spellings.

   Burke uses *revolution* in a Fortune's wheel context where he sees Marie Antoinette in a 'delightful vision': 'glittering like the morning-star, full of life, and splendor, and joy. Oh! What a revolution! and what an heart must I have, to contemplate without emotion that elevation and that fall!' (p. 169). The other uses of the word can be found on page 99 and, indeed, passim.

2. G. M. Trevelyan, *The English Revolution 1688-1689*, Oxford: Home University Library 1950 (first published 1938), pp. 11-12.

3. Quoted from Marilyn Butler, ed., *Burke, Paine, Godwin, and the Revolution Controversy*, Cambridge: Cambridge University Press, 1984, repr. 1988, pp. 31-32. Compare Burke's *Reflections*, p. 157.
   For those who want to sample the debate on the Revolution, Professor Butler's book is a very useful anthology.

4. Harold J. Laski, *Political Thought in England. Locke to Bentham*, London: Oxford University Press, 1961 (first published 1920), pp. 147-149. This was written when Laski was in his mid-twenties, in his pre-socialist days.

5.   William Doyle, *The Oxford History of the French Revolution*, Oxford: Oxford University Press, 1989, p. 425.
   There are several paperback editions of selections from Burke's works, among them B.W. Hill, ed., *Edmund Burke On Government, Politics and Society*, Fontana/ The Harvester Press, 1975. Also Iain Hampsher-Monk, ed., *The Political Philosophy of Edmund Burke*, London: Longman, 1987.
   C. B. Macpherson's *Burke* (Past Masters series), Oxford: Oxford University Press, 1980, is a good short introduction.
   William Hazlitt opened his essay 'On the Character of Burke' (1807) with the words: 'There is no single speech of Mr. Burke which can convey a satisfactory idea of his powers of mind: to do him justice, it would be necessary to quote all his works; the only specimen of Burke is, *all that he wrote*'.

Tom Paine:
Citizen of the World

Mel Leiman

Tom Paine was probably the only person in the world who was an 'on the spot' active agitator for both the American Revolution and the French Revolution. Like all writers, Paine's thinking was shaped as well as limited by the socio-political environment in which he lived, but unlike the vast majority, he had a powerful effect in influencing that environment. Although the main focus of this paper is the relationship of Paine and the French Revolution, it is useful to start with his earlier writings on the American Revolution since several of the themes are interwoven in his two principal works, *Common Sense* and *Rights of Man*.

In a fundamental way, Paine considered himself a citizen of the world, spreading the message of reason and revolution. In *Rights of Man*, he stated:

> I speak an open and disinterested language, dictated by no passion but that of humanity ... Independence is my happiness, and I view things as they are, without regard to place or person; my country is the world, and my religion is to do good.[1]

Paine's incendiary pamphlet *Common Sense*, which appeared in January 1776 several months after armed conflict had broken out between British and colonial soldiers at Lexington and Concord, had the impact of a best seller on the American colonies. Scholars estimate that at least 150,000 copies were sold. Most of the colonists at this time were still wavering between

The Dolphin 19
©Aarhus University Press 1990

demanding separation from England and hoping that England would make sufficient compromises to maintain colonial relationship with the mother country.

After years of asserting modest authority in colonial life, the British government, under economic and political pressure from its merchant class, introduced a series of highly unpopular taxes on the colonists. In doing this, the British were following standard guidelines of mercantilist theory by using the colonies to further the interests of the mother country, as interpreted by the dominant statesmen. In practice, this translated as encouraging those economic activities in the colony that dovetailed with the interests of the controlling country and prohibiting those that did not do so. The British effort to assert their economic muscle led to colonial boycotts of British goods, destruction of British property, intimidation of British tax collectors, engagement in smuggling to evade British laws, and eventually armed force against British troops sent to quell colonial resistance.

In clear and strident terms, Paine urged the colonists to declare their immediate independence from England, and to cease looking for some way of reconciling the interests of the two countries. What Paine's writings lacked in sophistication and scholarliness was more than overcome by the forthright populist rhetoric readily understood by the masses of people. He drew a dramatic contrast between the decadent and oppressive aristocratic order of Europe and the democracy of the new world. He saw America as a land with unlimited economic opportunities once the yoke of colonialism was lifted and representative democracy replaced absolute monarchy. As the pre-eminent voice of American idealism Paine could say that 'America's independence ... will usher in a new era in world history ... We have it in our power to begin the world over again.'[2] Paine was a messianic visionary rather than a meticulous historian carefully weighing the accumulated grievances of the American colonists. As a twentieth century critic stated:

Paine's pamphlet [*Common Sense*] was no mere recital of ministerial blunders, no learned disquisition on constitutional or imperial theory. His readers were summoned to greatness, recruited for a crusade against the old world and the values from which so many Americans had fled.[3]

Although aware of class differences within colonial America, Paine seemed to view this as a secondary phenomenon. So intent was he to mount a crusade against European monarchies that he naively stated: 'There [in America] the poor are not oppressed, the rich are not privileged ... There taxes are few because the government is free.'[4] The truth was rather that by the eve of the Revolutionary War, political and economic life in the colonies was dominated by powerful merchants and large landholders, particularly in the slaveholding South.

In his effort to stress the exploitation of America by England and the negative role of an authoritarian state *vis-à-vis* its citizens and foreign colonists, Paine understated the importance of domestic class conflict. For him, government posed a key threat to life, liberty and property, and thus its only proper role was to provide a setting for free market activities. Strong government operating in the interest of privileged wealthy strata was the enemy of liberty and economic progress.

Paine shared Adam Smith's vision in *The Wealth of Nations*, published in 1776, of a competitive self-regulating economy in which rational people seeking to advance their self-interest unintentionally furthered the social interest of society. Mercantile restrictions were thus seen as an 'engine of oppression' by a small number of monopolistic merchants - political influence with the monarchy enabled them to acquire monopoly privileges - against the vast majority of consumers. As Eric Foner said, 'Paine envisioned a society in which representative government with a written constitution together with economic growth would produce social harmony, equality [of opportunity] and an economic abundance in which all classes would share.'[5] Monarchy, on the other hand, resulted in political oppression and corruption as well as war and excessive taxation of the poor and middle ranks of the population.

Within the context of his era, Paine was correct in thinking that the wide (although unequal) diffusion of property in early America enabled large numbers of people - slaves, of course, were the exception - to exercise political rights. The wider issue of the compatibility of capitalism and democracy will be dealt with at the end of this article.

This American phase of Paine's life was highly successful. His full-fledged participation in the American War of Independence against the world's most powerful economic and military force gave his name a special aura of patriotism. Who can forget his famous words of encouragement to the beleaguered armies of Washington in the early years of the revolutionary struggle?

These are the times that try men's souls. The summer soldier and the sunshine patriot will, in this crisis, shrink from the service of his country; but he that stands it now, deserves the love and thanks of man and woman. Tyranny, like hell, is not easily conquered; yet we have this consolation with us, that the harder the conflict, the more glorious the triumph. What we obtain too cheap, we esteem too lightly: it is dearness only that gives everything its value.[6]

Paine returned to England in 1787, two years before the outbreak of the French Revolution, a revolution that thoroughly transformed the political scene of Europe. He became a key figure in English intellectual and radical circles, whose embrace of the French Revolution elicited a vigorous denunciation from the British conservatives. These Britishers began to see the abolishment of feudal property in France as a potential threat to the British monarchy.

Edmund Burke's *Reflections on the Revolution in France*, published in November 1790, set the tone. It was nothing less than a tirade against revolutionary social change. His conservative *weltanshauung* conditioned him to regard French events as the triumph of anarchy over reason and the slow accumulation of past wisdom. Revolution tears asunder the fragile structure of society. Burke was not averse to gradual, modest changes that kept the basic structure intact, but beyond that, chaos and destructiveness were seen as likely results. He could thus reconcile upholding the English Revolution of 1688 while denouncing the French Revolution of 1789. A stable society required an acceptance of order, discipline and inequality:

> Good order is the foundation of all good things. To be enabled to acquire, the people, without being servile, must be tractable and obedient. The magistrate must have his reverence, the laws their authority. The body of the people ... must respect that property of which they can not partake. They must labor to obtain what by labor can be obtained; and when they find, as they commonly do, the success disproportioned to the endeavour, they must be taught their consolation in the final proportions of eternal justice.[7]

Burke's defense of aristocratic institutions, as well as his attack on the French Revolution, was thus linked to the vague generalities of 'eternal justice'. Is it any wonder that some people would harbor the subversive thought that 'eternal justice' begins in the here and now? Paine's powerful *Rights of Man* was specifically aimed at refuting Burke's treatise, which he regarded as 'an outrageous abuse on the French Revolution and the principle of liberty.'[8]

Part 1 appeared in March 1791 and Part 2 the following year. They had the same powerful impact on the British (particularly among the intellectual radicals and urban artisans and perhaps in the embryonic working class movement) that the earlier *Common Sense* had on the Americans. In the sharply repressive atmosphere of the 1790s, Paine was charged with seditious writing and escaped to France to avoid imprisonment.

Rights of Man is a more impressive work than *Common Sense*, although its political impact was much less. Paine continued the basic theme that the British system of monarchy and hereditary privilege was unjust, corrupt and ineffective, and ought to be speedily replaced by a republican government, the only legitimate type of government. In dramatic contrast to Burke, Paine vindicated the French Revolution and defended the French National Assembly's *Declaration of the Rights of Man*. Paine had, in fact, been in close contact with the group that drew up this document.

While 'all hereditary government over a people [as in England] is to them a species of slavery ... the French constitution says that the law is the same to every individual, whether to protect or punish. All are equal in its sight.'[9] In response to Burke's defense of British monarchy, Paine pronounced that 'the splendor of a throne is no other than the corruption of the state. It is made up of a band of parasites, living in luxurious indolence, out of the public taxes.'[10] This monarchical system is strikingly inferior to a democratic republic that Paine says 'takes society and civilization for its basis; nature, reason, and experience, for its guide.'[11] A republic is, moreover, overwhelmingly likely, according to Paine who is echoing Adam Smith, to opt for mutually advantageous free trade rather than tariffs and subsidies, and for lower taxes.

Paine also believed that a world of free commerce would be a more peaceful one. The British philosopher A. J. Ayer correctly indicates the limitations of Paine's perspective:

> It is strange that it did not occur to Paine that it might be in the interest of manufacturers to promote wars, in order to obtain raw materials more cheaply, or acquire, even to the point of monopolizing, new markets for their goods.[12]

Paine was also a strong assailant of Britain's law of primogeniture (the system of property descending through the eldest son) that was supported by a combination of Whigs and Tories (e.g. Burke and Malthus) in the belief that it helped to preserve the basic social structure. To Paine, primogeniture laws were 'unnatural and unjust ... [and] by cutting off the younger children from their proper proportion of inheritance, the public is loaded with the expense of maintaining them.'[13] The reforms of the French Revolution specifically rejected primogeniture in favor of equal descent among the heirs.

As noted earlier, Paine played an active role in the political affairs of the French Revolution as well as in the intellectual life stimulated by it. Two strands of thought, converging and diverging at different times, acted on Paine. The early influence of Locke, with its stress on individualism, is too obvious to need elaboration. This led him in the direction of rejecting the monarchy and mercantilism in favor of representative government and the free market. He envisioned a replacement of the landed aristocracy by a society of small property holders.

His participation in the French Revolution exposed him to another influence, the circle around Condorcet and Godwin. These 'perfectibilists' believed that man's essentially good nature was corrupted by societal institutions. In particular, they were against the privileged class that used the state to further their own ends. Their ideal was a form of anarchical communism. They may well have helped to sensitize Paine to the poverty and inequality that tends to accompany the economic development process. This is reflected in the lengthy last chapter of *Rights of Man*, in which Paine revealed a strong social dimension to his thinking. He, in fact, foreshadowed the twentieth-century welfare state.

Paine worked out in considerable detail methods for ameliorating economic injustice in a European society characterized by severely unequal wealth and income distribution patterns. In a way that revealed what Eric Foner aptly calls Paine's 'radical cast of mind,'[14] Paine advocated the following far-sighted measures, which he emphasized were of the nature of rights and not of charity: annual payments to senior citizens over 50 and 60 years of age; welfare payments to the poor; allowances for education ('A nation under a well-regulated government should permit none to remain uninstructed'[15]); payments for the birth of a child; humane state-supported homes providing lodging, food and certain kinds of employment to the unemployed (including a cash payment to individuals on their departure from these work houses); and perhaps the most radical proposal: a progressive income tax with a built-in confiscatory level. The effect of this tax would be 'to extirpate the unjust and unnatural law of primogeniture, and the vicious influence of the aristocratical system'.[16] A major source of the surplus for paying for this welfare package would be reduced wasteful spending on the military. Paine's notion of putting limits on private property accumulation cut against the grain of mainstream economic thought until twentieth-century reformers gained prominence.

The outcome of Paine's struggle in the French Revolution was less successful than in the American Revolution.[17] He was swept up in the ebbs and flows of the complex, and often contradictory, socio-political changes in the French Revolution. The struggle for hegemony, in which the bourgeoisie eventually emerged triumphant, involved many shifting intraclass and interclass alliances and conflicts.[18] The moderate middle class group he supported, the Girondins, was ejected from power in mid-1793 by the Jacobins, the voice of the Parisian working class. Most went to the guillotine by the end of 1793, despite Paine's courageous effort to defend them. He had written to Danton that he was 'exceedingly disturbed at the distractions and jealousies, discontents that reign among us, and which, if they continue, will bring ruin and disgrace on the Republic.'[19] A plaintive letter to Thomas

Jefferson during this time also expressed his disappointment with the Revolution: 'Had this revolution been conducted consistently with its principles, there was once a good prospect of extending liberty through the greatest part of Europe; but I now relinquish that hope.'[20]

Paine himself was imprisoned for ten months (December 28, 1793 to November 4, 1794) and came within an eyelash of following his friends to the guillotine. He was saved by the intervention of James Monroe, the American ambassador to France, who also helped him to recover from an illness contracted in jail. Paine witnessed the decline of the Revolution from its democratic beginnings to a Reign of Terror that devoured not only the counter-revolutionaries who were attempting to restore the monarchy, but the children of the Revolution as well, including Danton, Marat, and Robespierre. Paine struggled to preserve the revolutionary gains after his release from prison and re-admission to the Convention, but in the ensuing reaction after Napoleon overthrew the Directory in 1799, he felt pressured to return to America.

Unfortunately for Paine, the America he returned to in 1802 was different from the America he had left in 1787. His last work, *The Age of Reason*, a Deist attack on orthodox Christianity and especially the notion of the Bible as revealed truth, offended believers. One historian said, 'The social ferment of those years [1776-1783] had been stilled by a federal Constitution and a federalist ideology which threw the balance of political and social power into the hands of the powerful and the well-to-do.'[21]

Paine died in 1809, less appreciated by his contemporaries than by a number of later radicals who thought of him as an originator of a radical protest movement. Foner provides an explanation:

> Paine's writings provided a vision of a good society, a definition of active citizenship, which helped inspire expressions of protest ranging from the labor movement of the 1830's to the Populists of the 1890's. Thus ... Paine's thought deeply affected the evolution of radicalism in nineteenth-century America.[22]

He adds that Paine's legacy was also felt in England where 'his writings inspired the birth of a working-class radicalism.'

History has proven that England's parliamentary system has not been as destructive of human liberty as Paine predicted, nor the American system as productive. Both have produced mixed results - periods of relative freedom and periods of relative repression, honesty at the government level co-existing with corruption, subsidies to the impoverished together with favors for the wealthy. This package indicates, above all, that ideology operates within the crucible of history and not within a vacuum. Paine was writing on the eve of the industrial revolution and could not possibly have foreseen the ensuing structural transformation of society. It is during the period of transition from mercantilism to competitive capitalism and the subsequent deepening of the latter, that capitalism can march in tandem with an extension of democracy. Rapid economic growth facilitates these mutual movements. What Paine, as well as Smith and the classical economists, did not anticipate was the later transition of competitive capitalism to monopoly capitalism on a global scale. This transition inevitably made the relationship of capitalism and democracy more tenuous.

Paine was staunchly in favor of equality of opportunity and could accept an amount of differentiation that reflected differences in talent, effort and frugality, but severe actual economic inequality resulting from the very market activities he applauded (as well as those coming from privileged positions in an autocratic society, which he detested), made him retreat from his *laissez-faire* principles and embrace many social welfare reforms.

Paine's egalitarian vision was more in contradiction with free market individualism than he realized, although in the context of a pre- or early Industrial Revolution setting, this contradiction was muted. Whereas today's welfare state is actually state supported capitalism with abundant evidence of collusion between government and corporate elites, Paine's welfare state represented an effort to create capitalism with a human face.

Notes

1. Thomas Paine, *Rights of Man* (New York: Penguin Classics, 1985 edition) p. 228. The original date of publication was March 13, 1791 for Part One and February 17, 1792 for Part Two.
2. Paine, *Common Sense* (New York: Penguin Classics, 1986 edition) p. 120. The original date of publication was January 10, 1776.
3. Isaac Kramnick, Introduction to Paine, *Common Sense*, p. 43.
4. Paine, *Rights of Man*, p. 167. Paine also added the idea that because no one lived under wretched conditions, there would be no reason to expect unrest or riots.
5. Eric Foner, Introduction to Paine, *Rights of Man*, p. 13, in: Philip Foner, ed., *The Complete Writings of Thomas Paine*, 2 volumes (New York: Citadel Press, 1945).
6. This was the first issue of sixteen *Crisis* papers that appeared between December 13, 1776 and December 9, 1783. See M. D. Conway and C. Putnam, eds., *The Writings of Thomas Paine* (New York, 1906) or Philip Foner's edition of *The Complete Writings*.
7. *Reflections on the Revolution in France* (New York: Penguin Classics, 1985 edition) p. 372. The original date of publication was November 1790. Also see A. J. Ayer's discussion in his *Thomas Paine* (London: Faber & Faber, 1988) pp. 56-71.
8. Paine, *Rights of Man*, p. 35.
9. Paine, *ibid.*, pp. 200-201.

10. Paine, *ibid.*, p. 203. Paine added, 'The aristocracy are not the farmers who work the land and raise the produce, but are the mere consumers of the rent; [they] exist only for lazy enjoyment' (p. 227).

11. Paine, *ibid.*, p. 175.

12. Ayer, *Thomas Paine*, p. 93. Ayer also notes on the same page: 'Paine's conception of monarchy tended to be feudal, and he persisted in locating the cause of wars exclusively in the pride and avarice of monarchs and of the aristocrats who mingled with them.'

13. Paine, *Rights of Man*, chapter 5.

14. Eric Foner, Introduction to Paine, *Rights of Man*, p. 22

15. Paine, *Rights of Man*, p. 245.

16. Paine. *ibid.*, pp. 258-259.

17. For discussions on Paine's interaction with events and persons in the French Revolution, see G. Spater, 'European Revolutionary, 1789-1809,' in Ian Dyck, ed., *Citizen of the World: Essays on Thomas Paine* (London: Christopher Helm, 1987), pp. 50-70, and Ayer, *Thomas Paine*, chapter 7.

18. An exploration of this important topic is beyond the scope of this paper. For a penetrating analysis of the changing social forces and the recent historiographic debates on the French Revolution, see Paul McGarr, 'The Great French Revolution,' *International Socialism*, number 43, June 1989, pp. 15-110. He makes the excellent point that participants in real social conflict are not always fully conscious of their class interests and actions to further it, and that there may be divisions within the dominant class over deepening or arresting the process of change.

19. Ayer, *Thomas Paine*, p. 124.

20. Ayer, *ibid.*, p. 121-122. One striking contradiction with the 'Rights of Man' principle of the French Revolution was the support of many French leaders for slavery in the colonies. Slavery was not abolished until 1794, and its abolition was due far more to slave uprisings than to changes in the political attitudes of metropolitan France. Paine, on the other hand, was consistently anti-slavery. He also was far more aware of gender inequality than most reformers of his era. He said that 'deeply ingrained and oppressing social prejudices remain which confront women minute by minute, day by day.' M. D. Conway, ed., *Writings of Thomas Paine*, vol. 2, p. 60.

21. Kramnick, Introduction to Paine, *Common Sense*, p. 36.

22. Foner, Introduction to Paine, *Rights of Man*, p. 21.

Jane Austen's Political Silence

John A. Dussinger

Even without the benefit of modern critical theory, which has celebrated the
arcane matters of 'empty spaces', 'deep structures', and other forms of
indeterminacy in language itself, Jane Austen knew with a writer's instinct
the eloquence of 'unheard melodies' and cultivated a narrative economy that
embarrassed Walter Scott into admitting privately his own 'Big Bow-wow'
strain.[1] Barring the discovery of a cache with some precious manuscript on
a scale that Catherine Morland had imagined, the Austen reader has only the
'unheard melodies' to ponder in her extant writing. One intriguing silence
regards the cataclysmic events across the English Channel during her forma-
tive years. Never once does Austen mention directly the French Revolution
or the Napoleonic Wars in her fiction and her remaining correspondence. For
the literary critic, what matters most, of course, is not so much her political
opinion - whether Jacobin or anti-Jacobin - but rather how her political
orientation may have helped shape the novels that we want to keep reading
until the end of time.

To judge by past commentary, Austen's silence about such momentous
historical happenings may be attributed to one or more of the following
causes: 1) a provincial's indifference toward the public world in general;
2) a comic novelist's aesthetic distancing of her story from local history; and
3) a late eighteenth-century woman writer's reluctance, or inability, to enter
into the discourse of patriarchal politics.

The Dolphin 19
©Aarhus University Press 1990

1. The Author as Recluse

Thanks to the past decade of Austen scholarship, the image of a secluded spinster indifferent to politics appears to be on the wane. Although only a little over thirteen and a half years old when the Bastille fell, Austen was hardly ignorant of the catastrophe on the Continent; and because of her family connections, especially with two brothers in the Royal Navy at the time of Trafalgar, she never had the luxury of forgetting about the Napoleonic Wars threatening her immediate family as well as nation. In dedicating her juvenile piece 'Jack and Alice' to Francis Austen, 'Midshipman on board his Majesty's ship the *Perseverance*,' the teen-aged Jane obviously showed her admiration of this brother in the military service just as she did later when her younger brother joined the navy. Park Honan remarks the subtle influence of this family loyalty on her writing: '[A]t nearly every point in her career as she worked on her stories between the 1790s and 1815, her interest in her brothers Frank and Charles and the naval war helped to save her as a novelist from the unreality of the novel form - its psychologically restricting emphasis on a few sets of characters in a near-vacuum'.[2] Instead of 'a certain "hot-house" atmosphere' in stories about heroines narrowly preoccupied with the uncertainties of courtship, Honan concludes, Austen's fiction usually implies that political, military, economic, and social events, no matter how apparently far off, have an important effect on the domestic scene.

Whatever Austen's specific opinions of the French monarchy might have been, we do know that some years before the outbreak of the Revolution, intimate reports of the social life under the *ancien régime* were available to her. Her lively cousin Eliza, daughter of her father's elder sister and a frequent visitor at Steventon, was married to a French aristocrat, Jean Capotte, Comte de Feuillide, who was guillotined during the Terror in 1794. 'As a comtesse married to an officer,' Honan remarks, Eliza 'acted in theatricals at Versailles, saw the French King and Queen, and wrote letters to her jealous cousin Phila Walter back at Ightham Parsonage near Sevenoaks' (Honan, 45). Eliza's letters described all the glitter of *soirées* at the Trianon, including details about Marie-Antoinette's and the King's lavish costumes. Eliza herself cultivated the aristocratic lady's flirtatious airs and like Lady Bertram hardly went anywhere without her pug dogs. While a guest of the Austens at Christmas, she was active in the family's theatricals performed in their barn and probably inspired the characters of Elizabeth Bennet and Mary Crawford.[3] It was no secret that the whole Austen family were staunch Tory royalists; and while at St. John's College, the Austen brothers Henry and James instituted the conservative Oxford weekly, *The*

Loiterer. As an avid reader of this periodical, Jane Austen was inspired to try her own hand at such parody as 'The History of England', which mixes ironic humor unevenly with sincere compassion for the betrayed Stuarts, persecuted Roman Catholics, and downtrodden poor.

One of Austen's most tantalizing allusions to the War, analyzed at length by Warren Roberts, occurs in a letter to Cassandra, 30 August 1805:

> Next week seems likely to be an unpleasant one to this family on the matter of game. The evil intentions of the Guards are certain, and the gentlemen of the neighbourhood seem unwilling to come forward in any decided or early support of their rights. Edward Bridges has been trying to arouse their spirits, but without success. Mr. Hammond, under the influence of daughters and an expected ball, declares he will do nothing.[4]

Jane was writing from Goodnestone Farm, only seven miles from the Kentish coast, while her sister was staying at their brother Edward's estate, Godmersham, a few miles southwest of Canterbury.

Ever since England declared war in 1803, Napoleon had been planning an invasion; but because of the British navy's strategy of blockading French ports, he was unable to gather together the flotilla needed. By the summer of 1805, after the Anglo-Russian-Austrian alliance, Napoleon had to abandon his invasion plans and concentrate on defeating his adversaries to the east. But while secretly withdrawing his troops from the west coast for this new development, he kept a sizeable force at Boulogne to delude the British into thinking an invasion was still imminent. As Roberts observes: 'To be at a Kent farm 7 miles from Deal in August 1805 was to be in a neighbourhood that for two years had lived under the threat of invasion. Austen could not have been uninformed of this menace' (Roberts, 83).

Evidently, then, Austen's oblique reference to the 'evil intentions of the Guards' mocks the unpatriotic attitude of some Kentish neighbours, who were more worried about being disrupted in their hunting and dancing parties than about being deprived of their 'rights' by an invading enemy (Roberts, 86). Even if there seems no reason to doubt that Austen knew firsthand the real dangers of the War, how to interpret her responses to it remains problematic.

2. The Principle of Aesthetic Distance

Without denying that Austen's avoidance of contemporary political issues in her novels was at least partly for the sake of achieving an aesthetic universality, we need to remember that her letters reveal a similar cryptic shorthand style toward public events. By 1796, the time of Austen's first extant letters, the executions of Louis XVI and Marie-Antoinette and the Terror had given way to the Directory, a relatively calmer government at home but still bent on continuing the wars with France's royalist neighbors. Austen's few laconic comments on the effects of Britain's war with France suggest a calculated method of reducing international affairs to a domestic dimension: 'Have you seen that Major Byng, a nephew of Lord Torrington is dead? - That must be Edmund' (*Letters*, 111). As Roberts observes: 'It seems that she mentioned this fallen officer only because he was the relative of someone else; moreover, she did not say that he was killed in battle, but rather that he "is dead". Discussing an officer's death in this way, she lifted the event out of its military context and thereby deprived it of its public significance' (Roberts, 88).

Again, in the midst of a letter full of neighborhood happenings, without ever naming the Battle of Albuera, Austen remarks tersely on the human toll involved: 'How horrible it is to have so many people killed! - And what a blessing that one cares for none of them!' (*Letters*, 286). Since *The Times* devoted several issues in May 1811 to this military engagement, it was apparently unnecessary to go into any detail about it to Cassandra; and Roberts kindly attributes this taut response to Austen's deep feelings (Roberts, 92). Lacking other contexts for comparison, however, as he admits, one could interpret the tone in other ways, even to the extent of finding the 'regulated hatred' that Mudrick and Harding have attributed to her. 'Regulated detachment', perhaps in imitation of Hume and Gibbon, seems closer to Austen's attitude, an ironic distance often clumsily attempted in her juvenilia but finally brought to perfection in *Emma*.[5]

Whatever the motives for her reticence toward the War, Austen's self-imposed censorship worked nicely into her artistic economy. For instance, her playful demurrer concerning *Pride and Prejudice* belies her principle of meaningful omission in relating a story: 'it wants to be stretched out here and there with a long chapter of sense, if it could be had; if not, of solemn specious nonsense, about something unconnected with the story; an essay on writing, a critique on Walter Scott, or the history of Buonaparte, or anything that would form a contrast, and bring the reader with increased delight to the playfulness and epigrammatism of the general style' (*Letters*, 299-300). The references to Walter Scott and Napoleon leave no doubt that the thought of 'stretching' her narrative with topical material at least had occurred to her and that if only for artistic reasons alone she decided against it.

While quoting the above letter, Claudia Johnson unaccountably infers that Austen did not like *Pride and Prejudice* as much as her readers have: 'To her its "playfulness and epigrammatism" appeared excessive and unrelieved.'[6] Even if the author had developed her narrative powers over the years since the novel's inception as 'First Impressions' in the 1790s and may have revised the story drastically before its publication in 1813, there is hardly any debate about her enthusiasm for her achievement here. 'None of her novels delighted Jane Austen more,' Honan observes, 'than *Pride and Prejudice*. Her lopping and cropping reduced some chapters to theatre and epigram, but she had developed her heroine's interior life with great care. She had shown how a person of strong feeling is to survive - and it is this that links *Pride and Prejudice* with her later novels' (Honan, 315). One could argue, furthermore, that in its historical context this brilliant foreground of the individual life against the lightly sketched outer world of the Regency period reveals a conservative faith in character to prevail over political and economic determinism.

3. The Woman Writer as Marginal Observer

As a woman within a politically conservative family, particularly during the reactionary years of the Pitt era, aside from the other reasons educed, Austen may have deliberately avoided commenting on large public issues to steer clear of male-oriented controversies. At times she appears to have felt a feminine weariness of all the hero worship associated with the War, especially after the national hysteria over the victory at Trafalgar: ' - Southey's Life of Nelson; - I am tired of Lives of Nelson, being that I never read any. I will read this however, if Frank is mentioned in it' (*Letters*, 345-346). Since her brother Frank himself was a great admirer of Nelson, in moments like this Austen seems to be carving out a feminine space for herself by denigrating the Man of the Hour.

Once we grant the obvious - that despite the differences in the cultural attitudes between the England of 1789 and 1989, probably *any* woman, having been conventionally excluded from a public role in the triumphs of the British Empire, would be inclined to moments of jealousy and resentment toward men in general - the question still remains what Austen actually contributed to this discourse on power relations. After describing the political differences between women novelists during Austen's creative years, Claudia Johnson argues that despite conservative or radical feints these writers felt 'in varying degrees too marginal as women in their society to idealize established power' (Johnson, xxiii). In contrast to such contemporary writers as Hannah More and Mary Wollstonecraft, who harangued their readers mercilessly, Jane Austen deliberately cultivated a narrative manner that eschews overt political comment to the extent that generations of readers could assume that the larger social issues did not really interest her.

Given Austen's wily elusiveness in the first place, after Marilyn Butler's rigidly doctrinaire version of an anti-Jacobin author,[7] it is perhaps not surprising that a feminist arrives on the scene to discover 'an enabling strategy' to 'rewrite the lexicon of conservative discourse and thereby to dismantle myths propounded by anti-Jacobin novelists without seeming necessarily to imply a Jacobin wish to see society radically reconstituted' (Johnson, xxv). Despite Johnson's welcome correction of Butler's whole notion that Austen's novels had a single-minded purpose of attacking French political radicalism, there is nevertheless a similar reductionist tendency in wanting to glorify the individualistic theme at the expense of the established community, an arrangement that probably reflects more the distortions of current ideology than early nineteenth-century attitudes. Johnson's rebuttal of Lionel Trilling's reading of the 'noble' life associated with the great houses in Austen's novels again emphasizes a vibrant individualism without regarding the author's explicit abhorrence of the delusions resulting from solitude. After much intelligent, if highly selective, reading, all that Johnson proposes against Butler's vigorously wrong-headed debate is a bland 'middle ground that had been eaten away by the polarizing polemics born of the 1790s' (Johnson, 166).

4. Mimesis as a Way of Knowing

An aesthetic transcendence of historical actuality as well as a feminine detachment from the male's political arena may have motivated Austen's silence about the noisy events of her brief lifetime. What remains to be considered, however, is her peculiar economy in representing anything at all, as if deliberately reminding us that the whole truth can never be revealed in language.

In general, to gain the effect of objectivity, description in eighteenth-century writing often assumes the model of the charade, providing certain designations without naming the thing itself. We see this most humorously in Swift, when the Lilliputians take an inventory of Gulliver's pockets and try to understand the meaning of his watch.[8] The periphrasis of Augustan 'poetic diction' similarly teases the reader into rethinking the nature of commonplace things, as for instance the simultaneous diminishing of the hunter's rifle and epic heightening of its power in Pope's *Windsor Forest*: 'He lifts the tube, and levels with his eye; / Straight a short thunder breaks the frozen sky'.[9] Although proper names for the various fish and fowl abound in the eighteenth-century georgic, such classically generic terms as 'scaly breed', 'finny tribe', and 'feathered kind' emphasize a static natural kingdom in contrast to the plenitude of individual species. Again, as if to suggest a cyclical universality, Gray's 'idle progeny' of Eton College 'succeed / To chase the rolling circle's speed, / Or urge the flying ball'.[10] The names of the particular games and their players may change, but their abstract functions remain the same through Eton's history. Finally, Gibbon's elaborate circumlocution in describing his birth is the verbal equivalent of the modern surgeon's rubber gloves: 'Decency and ignorance cast a veil over the mystery of generation, but I may relate that after floating nine months in a liquid element I was painfully transported into the vital air.'[11] At first glance one might suppose that such rhetorical figures are merely clever ways of avoiding prosaic denotation and thus anathema to any writer of realistic fiction; but on the contrary, by this metonymic practice the gifted Augustan writer can call attention to the epistemological assumptions buried in our conventional attitudes toward things identified by names and taken for granted.

Besides her wide reading in numerous eighteenth-century authors, from her early years Austen, we know, was fond of devising various charades and conundrums for the amusement of family members. Although in all her novels Austen's occasional narrative reflexivity draws attention to the contingencies of language and the incompleteness of the storytelling, it is in *Emma* that the 'ludic spirit' prevails. In the Highbury world not only Frank Churchill but almost everyone gets into the act of playing word games, even Mr. Woodhouse, who tries to recall the strangely erotic charade about 'Kitty, a fair but frozen maid.'[12] As the mature Austen fully recognized, 'Seldom, very seldom, does complete truth belong to any human disclosure; seldom can it happen that something is not a little disguised, or a little mistaken' (*Emma*, 431). From the context of this novel, the main reason for the problem of communication is the inherent human intentionality toward the other.

Austen's style implies the difficulty of knowing the real thing, the thing-in-itself. All that we ever know, to invoke Locke, are the ideas of our mind. Because it is at best an interposition of self and other, writing is bound to fall short of the actual experience represented and relies heavily on conventions of other texts to give coherence to what happened. How is one to comprehend the Revolution in France without ever having been there at the time? Austen's reply to James Stanier Clarke, the Royal Librarian, clarifies a writer's credo of describing only what one can possibly know firsthand and of avoiding merely fanciful representation.[13] Even under the worst circumstances of receiving letters from a rival in love, the authentic encoding of reality is preferable to mere chimeras, as Fanny Price reflects:

'There was great food for meditation in this letter, and chiefly for unpleasant meditation; and yet, with all the uneasiness it supplied, it connected her with the absent, it told her of people and things about whom she had never felt so much curiosity as now, and she would have been glad to have been sure of such a letter every week' (*Mansfield Park*, 394). A letter from Mary Crawford, painful as it is in intention, nevertheless has the power of connecting the reader with the absent world of Mansfield Park, which at this moment is emotion recollected in tranquillity. But writing about something not experienced lacks this power of recollection, and maybe for this reason more than anything else Austen chose to remain silent about the cataclysmic events in a world only a few miles off the Kentish coast.

In *Northanger Abbey*, probably her first completed novel, we see the same concern with how the individual mind can take in historical truth by means other than borrowed texts, many times removed from actual events. With luck, however, even imaginary representations may offer insights as Catherine Morland alights on the potential evil of General Tilney; and when the visions of romance are over, she still has to confront the no less mysterious workings of the political and economic system that involves the woman as pawn in marriages of power relationships.

It is this double awareness that visions of reality are stranger than visions of romance that escapes comment in the narrative while Henry talks for victory over poor Catherine after discovering her suspicions of his father's responsibility for his mother's death: 'Remember the country and the age in which we live. Remember that we are English, that we are Christians. Consult your own understanding, your own sense of the probable, your own observation of what is passing around you - Does our education prepare us for such atrocities? Do our laws connive at them? Could they be perpetrated without being known, in a country like this, where social and literary intercourse is on such a footing; *where every man is surrounded by a neighbourhood of voluntary spies, and where roads and newspapers lay every thing open*?' (*Northanger Abbey*, my emphasis, 197-198). If Henry's disabusing Catherine of her illusions comes at the heavy price of reminding her that their country has given up individual liberties in reaction to the political threat on the other side of the English Channel, we can also suspect that an irresistible smile is coming upon the author's face as she contemplates this scene of male and national chauvinism, which both quietly assumes the woman's silence as the order of things and blindly accepts governmental repression as a token of progressive society.

Notwithstanding the recent feminist stress on the woman's exclusion from the political sphere, we need to keep in mind Austen's discriminating sense of what can and cannot be represented adequately. The immediate confrontation between Catherine and Henry over the improbability of any murderous intentions in an *English* patriarch as opposed to their French or other Latin counterparts, given the overall context, is finally a laughable disclosure of a political truth that no one, neither the privileged male spokesman nor the omniscient narrator, is willing to interpret. To judge by Austen's pixie role toward her readers as well as characters while her novels approach closure, some things are best left unsaid.

Notes

1. 'Also read again, and for the third time at least, Miss Austen's very finely written novel of *Pride and Prejudice*. That young lady had a talent for describing the involvements and feelings and characters of ordinary life, which is to me the most wonderful I ever met with. The Big Bow-wow strain I can do myself like any now going; but the exquisite touch, which renders ordinary commonplace things and characters interesting, from the truth of the description and the sentiment, is denied to me.' Walter Scott, *Journal*, 14 March 1826, quoted from Ian Watt's introduction to *Jane Austen*, Twentieth Century Views (Englewood Cliffs, N.J.: Prentice-Hall, 1963), p. 3.

2. Park Honan, *Jane Austen: Her Life* (New York: St. Martin's Press, 1987), p. 224. All further references to this work included in parentheses within the text.

3. Besides her husband's social rank and her Austenian loyalties, Eliza would have further reason to take the Tory side during the long Warren Hastings trial, when the liberal Whigs were castigating her godfather (Honan, 43-44). Since there is a suspicion that Mrs. Philadelphia Hancock, while married to a surgeon about twenty years older than herself, became Hastings's mistress, it is also possible that Eliza was the natural daughter of the Governor-General of Bengal. Such a relationship would account for the £10,000 trust fund Hastings set up for Eliza.

4. *Jane Austen's Letters to her Sister Cassandra and Others*, ed. R.W. Chapman, 2nd edition (Oxford: Oxford University Press, [1952] reprinted 1979), p. 169. Warren Roberts, *Jane Austen and the French Revolution* (New York: St. Martin's Press, 1979), pp. 80-88. Further references to Austen's *Letters* and to Roberts are to these books, respectively, included in parentheses within the text.

5. See D. W. Harding, 'Regulated Hatred: An Aspect of the Work of Jane Austen', *Jane Austen*, ed. Ian Watt (Englewood Cliffs, N.J.: Prentice-Hall, 1963), pp. 166-179, and Marvin Mudrick, *Jane Austen: Irony as Defense and Discovery* (Princeton, N.J.: Princeton University Press, 1952). While arguing that Jane Austen sought detachment in writing about the contemporary world, Roberts misses the opportunity of comparing her stylistic aim with some of the major historical writers in the eighteenth century. For example, on Hume's ideal of detachment as a defense against the treacherous vicissitudes of one's personal life, see my article, 'David Hume's Denial of Personal Identity: The Making of a Skeptic', *American Imago*, 37 (1980), pp. 334-350. For a capacious view of the epistemological implications of this narrative stance, see Leo Braudy, *Narrative Form in History and Fiction* (Princeton: Princeton University Press, 1970).

6. Claudia L. Johnson, *Jane Austen: Women, Politics, and the Novel* (Chicago and

London: University of Chicago Press, 1988), p. 73.

7. Marilyn Butler, *Jane Austen and the War of Ideas* (Oxford: Clarendon, 1975, reprinted 1976).

8. 'We directed him to draw out whatever was at the end of that chain; which appeared to be a globe, half silver, and half of some transparent metal: for on the transparent side we saw certain strange figures circularly drawn, and thought we could touch them, until we found our fingers stopped with that lucid substance. He put this engine to our ears, which made an incessant noise like that of a watermill. And we conjecture it is either some unknown animal, or the god that he worships; but we are more inclined to the latter opinion, because he assured us (if we understood him right, for he expressed himself very imperfectly), that he seldom did any thing without consulting it. He called it his oracle, and said it pointed out the time for every action of his life.' Jonathan Swift, *Gulliver's Travels*, Part I, chapter 2.

9. Alexander Pope, 'Windsor Forest', ll. 129-130.

10. Thomas Gray, 'Ode on a Distant Prospect of Eton College', ll. 28-30.

11. *The Autobiography of Edward Gibbon*, ed. Dero A. Saunders (New York: Meridian Books, 1961), p. 52.

12. *Emma*, in *The Novels of Jane Austen*, ed. R.W. Chapman, Five Volumes, Third Edition (London: Oxford University Press, 1933, reprinted 1960), IV, 78-79. Further references to Austen's novels are to this edition, in parentheses within the text.

13. 'You are very very kind in your hints as to the sort of composition which might recommend me at present, and I am fully sensible that an historical romance, founded on the House of Saxe Cobourg, might be much more to the purpose of profit or popularity than such pictures of domestic life in country villages as I deal in. But I could no more write a romance than an epic poem. I could not sit seriously down to write a serious romance under any other motive than to save my life; and if it were indispensable for me to keep it up and never relax into laughing at myself or other people, I am sure I should be hung before I had finished the first chapter. No, I must keep to my own style and go on in my own way; and though I may never succeed again in that, I am convinced that I should totally fail in any other' (*Letters*, 126-127).

The Fires of Orc
William Blake and the Rhetoric of Revolutionary Discourse

Ib Johansen

> Fiery the Angels rose, & as they rose deep thunder roll'd
> Around their shores: indignant burning with the fires of Orc
> ...
> They slow advance to shut the five gates of their law-built heaven
> Filled with blasting fancies and with mildews of despair
> With fierce disease and lust, unable to stem the fires of Orc;
> But the five gates were consum'd, & their bolts and hinges melted
> And the fierce flames burnt round the heavens, & round the abodes of men
>
> William Blake: *America a Prophecy* (1793)

> ... Says Reason directly, - *'Beware of wolves in sheeps' clothing - Hypocrites -*
> *Robbers, Murderers, Fellows void of Principle. - Incendiaries* who would set fire
> to a house, that they might plunder the property in the confusion ...'
>
> *Liberty and Property Preserved Against Republicans and Levellers,*
> Number II (1792)

1. Rhetoric and Power

The English debate on the French Revolution was also a controversy over language, i.e. over the political and social function of linguistic and rhetorical codes, over the rights and obligations of language-users, etc. What was at stake was no less than the political control of language itself - or, to put it another way, the efficiency (and legitimacy) of *rhetorical power*. According to Stephen Prickett (referring to Olivia Smith's book on the revolution debate in England *The Politics of Language 1791-1819* (1984)),

One reason for the massive influence of Burke's *Reflections* on the entire subsequent debate was simply that he had at the outset occupied the linguistic high ground, taking over the language of the Bible and of nature for his case in such a way that anyone who wished to take issue with him was disadvantaged right from the start by being made to appear atheistical, anti-religious and unnatural ... Many radical pamphleteers of the 1790s were evidently constrained by a feeling that, since they lacked Burke's education and superb command of the language, their 'plain speech' could carry neither the weight nor the implied historical consensus of his judgement.[1]

This point of view may be disputed, of course, and Prickett himself points out that 'the exceptions are too numerous and powerful for the case to carry total conviction'.[2] He emphasizes that, as a matter of fact, a number of radical writers were *not* culturally overawed by Burke, and 'If the first generation of radical apologists eventually lost the argument with Burke, it was more due to the excesses of the Revolution itself than to any inherent cultural bias of the English language' (this is *also* a point that may be disputed).[3] Furthermore, according to the political philosophy of Edmund Burke, the communicative interaction between the spokesmen of the conservative Establishment and the lower classes could not possibly be brought about, insofar as the latter were not supposed to possess the *linguistic competence* needed for such an exchange: '... conservative pamphleteers could not address their readers [the 'swinish multitude'] as intelligent persons because to do so would deny the major justification for the subordination of the audience. Subordination could not be intellectually explained to a body of people who were excluded from political discussion on the grounds of their irrationality' (Olivia Smith).[4] In this perspective communication between the Establishment and the masses would seem to be an altogether futile project - it would not even be an example of one-way communication, but rather a *rhetorical effort with no addressee*. The 'linguistic high ground' occupied by Burke and his fellow-conservatives - 'The temple of honour ... seated on an eminence'[5]- by its very definition prevented the message from ever leaving the enchanted circle of the speakers; everything must remain within the closed circuit of this interpretive community (on the *other* side of a kind of semiotic 'event horizon').

But at the same time writers like Hannah More and organizations like the Association for Preserving Liberty and Property against Republicans and Levellers tried to *popularize* the conservative message and remind the lower orders of 'their vulnerability to their own violence, illness, the birth of too many children, ignorance, and bankruptcy; and of the gratitude that they owe to English society and to the government for whatever security they have'.[6] The conservatives were not wholly successful in monopolizing 'the language of the Bible and of nature' (Prickett). E.P. Thompson has shown to what extent the Dissenting tradition influenced political radicalism in England at the end of the eighteenth and the beginning of the nineteenth centuries - it was omnipresent as 'one of the elements precipitated in the English Jacobin agitation'.[7] In *The Rise and Dissolution of the Infidel Societies in this Metropolis* (London, 1800) William Reid emphasizes the relationship between the tenets and beliefs of various sects and seceding chapels on the one hand and subversive political activity on the other. Among other groups Reid refers to 'a pretty numerous circle, near Hoxton, among a kind of *Infidel Mystics*, known to strangers ... by the appellation of *Ancient Deists* ... Here human learning was declaimed against ... and dreams, visions, and immediate revelations were recommended as a substitute ...'.[8] And yet, 'there was so little of real religion in their composition, that it almost immediately yielded to the stronger impulse of the French Revolution, and terminated in the general conversion of the members into *politicians* and *inquirers after news*'.[9] In Reid's conservative perspective any kind of religious 'enthusiasm' is fraught with the dangers of political insubordination, for

> under the idea of the instrumentality of the French revolution, in the fulfilment of prophecies, religion itself became accessary to deism and atheism! Prophecies, relative to the destruction of almost every kingdom and empire in the world, teemed from the British press, some of them in weekly numbers ...[10]

As E.P. Thompson puts it, 'Against [this] background of London dissent, with its fringe of deists and earnest mythics, William Blake seems no longer the cranky untutored genius that he must seem to those who know only the genteel culture of the time. On the contrary, he is the original yet authentic voice of a long popular tradition'.[11]

Richard Price's *A Discourse of the Love of Our Country* (1789) also belongs to this tradition. Furthermore, it was this lecture (given on 4 November 1789 to The Society for Commemorating the Revolution in Great Britain) that provoked Edmund Burke to write a reply in his *Reflections* (1790), thus inaugurating the whole debate on the French Revolution in England. The rhetoric of Price's treatise is characterized by its Biblical echoes and phraseology, and these features become very conspicuous near the end of his speech:

> What an eventful period is this! I am thankful that I have lived to it; and I could almost say, *Lord, now lettest thou thy servant depart in peace, for mine eyes have seen thy salvation* [cf. Luke 2,29-30]. I have lived to see a diffusion of knowledge, which has undermined superstition and error - I have lived to see the rights of men better understood than ever; and nations panting for liberty, which seemed to have lost the idea of it. - I have lived to see THIRTY MILLIONS of people, indignant and resolute, spurning at slavery, and demanding liberty with an irresistible voice;

their king led in triumph, and an arbitrary monarch surrendering himself to his subjects ... Behold, the light you have struck out, after setting AMERICA free, reflected to FRANCE, and there kindled into a blaze that lays despotism in ashes, and warms and illuminates EUROPE![12]

According to the American historian Lynn Hunt, the first months of the Revolution were dominated by 'the "generic plot" of comedy', i.e. the rhetoric of revolutionary discourse tended to focus on a conflict 'dividing a son who wants freedom from his more arbitrary and conventional father':

> In the plot of comedy, the 'blocking characters' (the father, in France, the king) are usually reconciled rather than repudiated altogether. The final reconciliation, the happy emergence of the new society, is signalled by a festive ritual, which often takes place at the end of the action.[13]

Richard Price thematizes a similar 'festive' mood in his peroration. The 'blocking' character (the King) is 'led in triumph', and he has voluntarily given himself up/over to his subjects, here representing the 'irresistible' vitality of a new generation, 'THIRTY MILLIONS of people, indignant and resolute, *spurning at slavery*, and demanding *liberty* ...'. The 'arbitrary monarch' is 'reconciled rather than repudiated altogether', insofar as he seems to participate *in the birth of 'the new society'*, i.e. to accept it and (even) lend it his support. The euphoric mood dominating Price's discourse, and the quasi-ceremonial style he has adopted in his speech (e.g. 'I have lived ... I have lived ... I have lived ...'), also fit in with his adherence to 'the "generic plot" of comedy'. The metaphorical references to the element of fire, however, point in the direction of the somewhat more destructive potentials inherent in the revolutionary set-up - 'despotism' cannot be accommodated to the revolutionary ethos but has to be laid 'in ashes', i.e. there is no way of submitting institutionalized tyranny to any kind of Hegelian *Aufhebung*, any rehabilitation programme. In the long run it appears that the 'law-built heaven' of the European monarchs is unable 'to stem the fires of Orc' - to use Blake's phrase in *America a Prophecy* (E 56).

The father-son conflict thematized in a number of texts attempting to interpret the events of the revolutionary era may be construed as an oedipal (or quasi-oedipal) conflict. In Price's speech the reference to the child Jesus in the temple ('Lord, now lettest thou thy servant depart in peace ...', etc.) suggests the emergence of the revolutionary 'brother horde' as a kind of 'secular saviour', whereas Burke stresses the *parricidal* characteristics of the members of the National Assembly in France, i.e. 'those children of their country who are prompt rashly to hack that aged parent in pieces, and put him into the kettle of magicians, in hopes that by their poisonous weeds, and wild incantations, they may regenerate the paternal constitution, and renovate their father's life'.[14] Burke is here clearly speaking on behalf of an 'enlightened' élite - paying lip-service to the project of Enlightenment, as it were, insofar as he characterizes his opponents as superstitious adherents to what Freud has termed 'the old, animistic conception of the universe'.[15] The practices of Burke's 'magicians', on the other hand, also recall Freud's description in *Totem and Taboo* of the psychological make-up of the 'brother horde' *after* the killing of the primordial father: 'The violent primal father had doubtless been the feared and envied model of each one of the company of brothers: and in the act of devouring him they accomplished their identification with him, and each one of them acquired a portion of his strength ...'.[16] Burke's cannibalistic imagery (cf. the reference to 'the kettle of magicians') perpetrates a *grotesque* version of the Freudian 'story' - a sarcastic comment on the optimistic ethos of a revolutionary discourse dominated by 'the "generic plot" of comedy'.

2. *The Marriage of Heaven and Hell*

The oedipal pattern may also be discerned in a number of Blake's texts. According to Ronald Paulson,

> Light, youth, sexuality join in Blake's image of revolution, and these are of course the images of revolt he develops with so light a touch in *Songs of Innocence and Experience* (the combined work), where the 'innocence' of the Biblical lambs and children Christ suffers to come unto Him is overdetermined by the growing sense of 'innocence' in the newborn, unfettered, unexperienced, and so (to his parents) dangerous child of the newborn American and French revolutions.[17]

In 'A Song of Liberty', the prophetic poem placed at the end of Blake's Menippean satire *The Marriage of Heaven and Hell* (1790-93), an oedipal struggle between a tyrant-father and a rebel-son is set forth in a series of dramatic images (echoing, by the way, Milton's portrayal of the Fall of Satan and his Angels in the first book of *Paradise Lost*). The woman (Jocasta) is present in this poem as 'The Eternal Female' (E 43), giving birth to her 'son of fire' (E 44) in the very first line and afterwards seemingly more or less identified with her *reproductive* role as a 'shadowy' female, unable to mediate between father and son in the ensuing conflict:

7. In her trembling hands she took the new born terror howling:

8. On those infinite mountains of light now barr'd out by the atlantic sea, the new born fire stood before the starry king!

9. Flag'd with grey brow'd snows and thunderous visages the jealous wings wav'd over the deep.

(E 43)

The confrontation between 'the new born fire' and 'the starry king' becomes a life-and-death struggle where the latter gives in to his *filicidal* impulses and 'hurls' his son into empty space:

10. The speary hand burned aloft, unbuckled was the shield, forth went the hand of jealousy among the flaming hair, and hurl'd the new born wonder thro' the starry night.

11. The fire, the fire, is falling!

(E 43)

But the downfall of the son is followed immediately afterwards by the fall from power of the father (who has 'hurled' him to the ground from an immense altitude). The destructive impulses released at this critical moment thus turn out to be 'filicidal' as well as 'patricidal' - destructive as well as *self*-destructive. The father's attempt to destroy his own son leads to the ruinous downfall of 'the jealous king' as well as his whole retinue ('... his grey brow'd counsellors, thunderous warriors, curl'd veterans, among helms, and shields, and chariots[,] horses, elephants: banners, castles, slings and rocks ...,' E 43); i.e. the fall of the tyrant entails the wholesale abolition of the political system he stands for (= the *ancien régime*). The haphazard enumeration of the *disjecta membra* of this system may also recall Milton's reference to 'the Conqueror' in the celestial battle (God), who according to Satan 'now beholds / Cherube and Seraph rouling in the Flood / with scattered *Arms* and *Ensigns* ...'[18] Insofar as the destructive potentials of the father-son conflict are stressed in 'A Song of Liberty', the overall ethos of the text - in contrast to *The Marriage of Heaven and Hell* as a whole - seems to be no longer determined by 'the "generic plot" of comedy', but rather by another plot-structure, i.e. that of *romance*. According to Lynn Hunt, this was the predominant narrative model used to interpret the events of the revolution in its *radical* phase, especially after the declaration of the Republic in September 1792:

Republicans in 1792 and 1793 emphasized the titanic nature of their struggle to free France, their distance from the past, the virtues of their efforts, and the utter villainy of their opponents. There was no longer one happy family, but there was still great confidence in the ability of republicans to remold France in the image of virtue.[19]

48

The rhetoric of this phase is dominated by allusions to 'those virtues so characteristic of romance: daring, courage, and headlong movement'.[20] The turbulent imagery of Blake's prophetic poem reflects this predilection for precipitate ('headlong') movement on the part of the authorial 'voice' of the text, culminating in the triumphant defiance of 'the son of fire' (another version of Blake's arch-rebel Orc) vis-à-vis his autocratic opponent, the latter representing the *ancien régime* as well as the tyranny of Old Testament law:

> 20. Spurning the clouds written with curses, [stamping] the stony law to dust, loosing the eternal horses from the dens of night ...
>
> (E 44)

In what other ways does Blake attempt to come to terms with (or what other strategic devices does he employ to re-present) the French Revolution in *The Marriage of Heaven and Hell*? *The Marriage* may be categorized as a Menippean satire (cf. Harold Bloom: '*The Marriage of Heaven and Hell* is a miniature "anatomy", in Northrop Frye's recently formulated sense of the term, and reserves to itself the anatomy's peculiar right to mingle satire with vision, furious laughter with the tonal complexity involved in any projection of the four or more last things').[21] According to Mikhail Bakhtin the menippea is by its very definition *subversive*, insofar as it attempts to turn upside down (or to use a more recent term, to 'deconstruct') any hierarchical structure, to 'carnivalize' any sacrosanct *order*; in textual terms it is characterized by its heterogeneity:

> The organic combination of philosophical dialogue, lofty symbol-systems, the adventure-fantastic, and slum naturalism is the outstanding characteristic of the menippea ... Dreams, daydreams, insanity destroy the epic and tragic wholeness of a person and his fate: the possibilities of another person and another life are revealed in him, he loses his finalized quality and ceases to mean only one thing; he ceases to coincide with himself.[22]

This seems to be a fairly accurate description of Blake's textual/narrative strategy in *The Marriage of Heaven and Hell*. For in this text Blake adopts a number of different genres and sets forth his 'message' by means of a *multiplicity of voices* - or perhaps it would be more accurate to say that the multiplicity of voices *is* the 'message', for in Blake's text man has also ceased 'to coincide with himself'. The climactic moment in Blake's *Marriage* thus occurs when an 'Angel' embraces a 'Devil' and through this *coincidentia oppositorum* or mystical 'marriage' is transformed into a prophet (later the Angel even undergoes a further transformation and ends up being 'a Devil'):

> When he [i.e. the Devil] had spoken: I beheld the Angel who stretched out his arms embracing the flame of fire and he was consumed and arose as Elijah.
> Note. This Angel, who is now become a Devil, is my particular friend: we often read the Bible together in its infernal or diabolical sense which the world shall have if they behave well
> I have also: The Bible of Hell: which the world shall have whether they will or no.

(E 43)

In *The Marriage of Heaven and Hell* Blake attempts to 'deconstruct' Christian orthodoxy (and even some more 'heterodox' versions of divinity such as, for example, Swedenborgian theosophy). He carries out this 'transvaluation of all values' not only by means of discursive - theological or anti-theological - reasoning, but also by means of a series of 'memorable fancies' (parodying Swedenborg's *memorabilia* or 'memorable relations' in his theo-logical writings), i.e. by means of what Bakhtin has termed 'the adventure-fantastic' ('We emphasize that the fantastic here serves not for the positive *embodiment* of truth, but as a mode for searching after truth, provoking it, and most important, *testing* it. To this end the heroes of Menippean satire ascend into heaven, descend into the nether world, wander through unknown and fantastic lands, are placed in extraordinary life situations ...').[23] In the first 'memorable fancy' the narrator of Blake's *Marriage of Heaven and Hell* manages to penetrate into the very centre of the Otherworld (a *descensus ad inferos* where the *persona* needs no guidance from a *psychopomp* such as the protagonist of Dante's *Divine Comedy* is provided with): 'As I was walking among the fires of hell, delighted with the enjoyments of Genius; which to Angels look like torment and insanity. I collected some of their Proverbs ...' (E 35). The narrator has become a freewheeling folklorist, a *flâneur* in Baudelaire's or Benjamin's sense ('Let the many attend to their daily affairs, the man of leisure can indulge in the perambulations of the *flâneur* only if as such he is already out of place ...')![24] The narrator in Blake's *Marriage* is precisely such a *displaced* character, and he carries out his deconstructive underground work by means of the Derridean strategy of 'reversal and displacement' (Gayatri Chakravorty Spivak).[25] In this way - by means of 'Dreams, daydreams, [and] *insanity*' - 'the epic and tragic wholeness of a person and his fate' is destroyed (Bakhtin). But it is only to 'Angels' (the representatives of Christian orthodoxy) that 'the enjoyments of Genius' look like 'torment and insanity' (E 35).

The *plot* in Blake's *Marriage* seems to follow a devious path - there is no attempt to establish a narrative order, a linear progression with a beginning, a middle, and an ending. The narratives - the five 'memorable fancies' - take us nowhere. Or rather: they take us everywhere - exploring the triple world of *heaven, earth,* and *hell* (in the classical menippea this cosmos consists of 'Olympus', 'earth', and 'the nether world').[26] It must be stressed, however, that the last (Fifth) Memorable Fancy does constitute a kind of peripety or *anagnorisis* or dramatic climax, insofar as the opposites of the text (heaven and hell, angel and devil) are here 'married' to each other (cf. the Angel 'embracing the flame of fire', E 42); this *hieros gamos* is followed in the subsequent 'Song of Liberty' by the pregnancy of 'The Eternal Female' and leads to the birth of the divine child-rebel or 'son of fire' mentioned above, i.e. Orc or the spirit of the French Revolution. The 'marriage' of textual (theological, philosophical, political, etc.) opposites thus turns out to be productive of further controversy or *Streit* - the comedy ending (where according to Northrop Frye 'Weddings are most common ...')[27] is put *under erasure*, as it were ... .

The metaphorics of *The Marriage of Heaven and Hell* centres on the revolutionary images of *cloud* and *fire* (cf. in Blake's *The French Revolution* [1791] the ambivalent use of the same elemental and cosmological symbolism, exemplified by for instance the reference to 'the *fiery cloud* of Voltaire, and *thund'rous* rocks of Rousseau', E 295, my italics). The opening lines of the text ('The Argument') from the very outset *encode* this symbolism, focusing (as it were) on its undecidability:

Rintrah roars & shakes his fires in the burdend air;
Hungry clouds swag on the deep

(E 33)

Whereas clouds in Blake's texts are very often associated with the forces of reaction, they seem in this context to be intimately linked up with the productive-destructive potentials of a revolutionary or proto-revolutionary situation. They impinge on the 'fires' shaken 'in the *burdend* air' by the enigmatic Rintrah (elsewhere in Blake's *oeuvre* an embodiment of prophetic wrath) - the very use of the word 'burdend' suggesting that a birth of some kind may be in the offing, possibly the birth of a 'new society' (cf. Frye on the *ethos* of comedy, stressing that 'the device in the plot that brings hero and heroine together causes a new society to crystallize around the hero ...').[28] Eventually, the Old World is relieved of its 'burden', i.e. its child or 'son of fire', in the final 'Song of Liberty', but at the same time it must be stressed that in 'The Argument' the 'burden' is rather a technical device, a *refrain* marking on a philosophical level the repetitive character of events in the 'cyclic' world of this versified - but as a matter of fact misleading - summary of the text (cf. Bloom's reference to the 'cyclic irony' of the opening poem).[29] When all is said and done, Rintrah is still suspended in mid-air with his destructive 'fires' (thunder-bolts) at the end of the poem, and the 'clouds' (the masses) are still 'Hungry'. In this context it may also be worthwhile recalling that thunder-and-lightning are essential as rhetorical stage-effects in the repertory of revolutionary language (they set forth in dramatic terms 'the sublime' of the revolution). According to Robespierre, the nations or the peoples of the world do not function as law courts, 'they do not pass sentences; they hurl the lightning ...'.[30] These thunderbolts, emanating from the collective 'body' of the people as a kind of spontaneous justice, reappear in Blake's mythopoetic rendering as 'the fires of Orc' in his prophetic poem *America* (1793).

The revolutionary thematics of *The Marriage of Heaven and Hell* manifests itself on other levels as well. The demonology or devil-lore of the whole satire may be related to contemporary attempts to 'demonize' plebeian agitators in general and the English Jacobins in particular. The ultra-conservative review *Liberty and Property Preserved Against Republicans and Levellers* thus refers to 'the Devil in the shape of Thomas Paine' and to the 'hellish doctrines' of the revolutionaries.[31] But occasionally, radical writers would turn these metaphorical weapons against those who used them, i.e. their conservative opponents. In Charles Pigott's *A Political Dictionary* (1795) it is thus asserted that 'A hard-working man and a poor Devil are synonimous in the language of Aristocracy',[32] and the plebeian pamphleteer Thomas Spence adopts a parodic stance in *The End of Oppression* (1795), when he envisages a 'political Millenium' where 'Hell from beneath does rise, / To meet thy lofty Eyes, / From the most pompous size, / How brought to nought'.[33] What Spence stages is a symbolic 'uncrowning' of the *theologus gloriosus* of the established church (and by implication of the whole ruling caste, the British *oligarchy*), and Blake employs a similar strategy in *The Marriage of Heaven and Hell* when he states at the beginning of the text (hinting at the year 1757, according to Swedenborg the year of the 'Last Judgment', but also the year of Blake's birth): 'As a new heaven is begun, and it is now thirty-three years since its advent: the Eternal Hell revives ...' (E 34). According to Jacques Derrida we must always go through a phase of *overturning* whenever we 'broach' a text; in this case the text that Blake 'broaches' is the Bible, and he reads the Bible in terms of a revolutionary politics and/or in terms of a series of 'demonic' effects, i.e. 'in its infernal or diabolical sense'. The phase of 'overturning' does justice to the fact that in a classical philosophical opposition we are ... dealing with ... a violent *hierarchy*. One of the two terms governs the other (axiologically, logically, etc.), or has the upper hand. To *deconstruct* the opposition, first of all, is to overturn the hierarchy at a given moment.[34]

In *The Marriage of Heaven and Hell* Blake's emphasis is on reversal rather than on displacement, on turning the world upside down rather than on reinterpreting its terms, or pushing them in new and unexpected directions (what Charles Levin identifies as the second moment of 'textual intervention', i.e. 'the sliding').[35]

What Blake attempts in *The Marriage* is to 'reverse' the hierarchical system of Christian-Platonic dualism, i.e. a system where 'One of the two [binary] terms' (good/evil, heaven/hell, reason/energy) undoubtedly 'governs the other ...', or has the upper hand'. The anti-Enlightenment drift of this rhetorical operation becomes obvious, when we consider to what extent the reason-energy polarity tends to dominate the discursive universe of the text, leaving the other binary oppositions in a subordinate position in terms of their structural 'power': '... Energy is the only life and is from the Body and Reason is the bound or outward circumference of Energy ...', and 'Those who restrain desire, do so because theirs is weak enough to be restrained; and the restrainer or reason *usurps* its place and *governs* the unwilling' (E 34, my italics). Blake translates this whole conceptual contest or *psychomachia* into more overtly mythical terms when he sets forth his own heterological version of the Fall of the Rebel Angels, revising Milton's orthodox account in *Paradise Lost*:

> It indeed appear'd to Reason as if Desire was cast out, but the Devils account is, that the Messiah fell. & formed a heaven of what he stole from the Abyss
>
> (E 34)

Instead of casting the Devil (*alias* 'Desire' *alias* 'Energy') in his archetypal role as arch-rebel - and as a Promethean thief of fire - the text on the contrary confounds high and low and God and Devil and incorporates these terms into a totally different theological 'language'. The Messiah becomes the demiurgic usurper in this pseudo-Gnostic account, but what he usurps is no longer taken from the *upper* but from the *nether* world, from 'the Abyss' or from what Bakhtin has termed 'the material bodily lower stratum' and Freud *the unconscious*.[36]

Narrative desire becomes synonymous with an attempt to subvert the epistemological prerogatives of our hegemonic culture, the 'grand narratives' of Western civilization. Or one kind of narrative power is played off against another (cf. '... but the Devils *account* is ...'). In this allegorical battle the terms turn out to be heavily politicized. According to William Reid, '... there is a natural correspondence between the lowest and worst passions in individual existence, and the tumultuous motions, the furor, or the panic fears of democracy in the great world ...', whereas 'Aristocracy ... naturally approximates to *Reason*'.[37] With more specific reference to the French Revolution Edmund Burke in his 'Remarks on the Policy of the Allies with Respect to France' (1793) stresses the 'dreadful and portentous *energy*' of the Jacobins. The Jacobins have *one* thing only 'to supply their innumerable defects': '- but that one thing is worth a thousand - they have *energy*'.[38] And in 'A Letter to William Elliott, Esq.' (1795) Burke explicitly classifies these energies as 'demonic': 'I knew that, attacked on all sides by the *infernal energies* of talents set in action by vice and disorder, authority could not stand upon authority alone ...'.[39] According to the UEA English Studies Group in their paper 'Strategies for Representing Revolution' the French are constantly 'portrayed as the carriers of desire, as those who are capable of taking up active, aggressive roles vis-à-vis the forces of history'.[40] Whereas the English are doomed to adopt a much more passive stance in this respect (the UES English Studies Group refers to 'spectatorial subject-positioning' as characteristic of the English attitude).[41] Only the French are capable of *acting out their desires* - the English can only *observe* and *talk* about what they see.

In *The Marriage of Heaven and Hell* this polarity between 'active, aggressive roles' on the one hand (the French) and 'spectatorial subject-positioning' on the other (the English) is transformed into the devil-angel polarity of the metaphysical framework of the text. This binary opposition is foregrounded and made particularly plain in the Fourth Memorable Fancy where the text reaches a narrative climax. Here the *persona* of the text wrestles with an Angel whose brimstone sermons represent a totally 'demonized' version of the Other, visualizing a subterranean 'Abyss, fiery as the smoke of a burning city' (E 40). According to Blake's angel companion the *persona*'s 'eternal lot' (E 40) is bound up with the appearance in this nether deep of a number of 'black and white spiders' (E 40) - and it is furthermore bound up with 'a cloud and fire' rolling through the deep 'blackning all beneath' (E 40, cf. the revolutionary connotations of these images). Finally, Leviathan itself ('a *monstrous* serpent', my italics, E 40) appears 'to the east, distant about three degrees' (E 40). The sublime of the revolution is thus turned into a *monstrosity* in accordance with Barbara Freeman's theory of monstrosity, insofar as she has pointed out that it is impossible to protect 'the *sublime* from the *monstrous* potential inherent in it'.[42] According to Martin K. Nurmi the whereabouts of Leviathan can be located rather precisely, for its position 'to the east, distant about three degrees' marks out its site as being 'Paris, which as Blake knew from his engravings in geographical books, was three degrees in longitude from London'.[43] It may further be added that Leviathan as an embodiment of revolutionary energy is later celebrated by Edward Rushton in his allegorical poem 'The Leviathan' (1806), where France is likened to a 'Leviathan' (i.e. a whale), wakening to a sense of its oppression when it feels the 'shaft' (harpoon) being driven into its flesh: 'Deep sinks the shaft, and now the people feel; / Pierced to the quick the tail soon mounts on high, / And splendour, wealth, and power, in one sad ruin lie'.[44] But the appearance of the revolutionary *numen* as Leviathan in the first place results from the Angel's particular *mis*reading of the situation, for as soon as the *persona*'s terrified companion has withdrawn 'into the mill' (E 40) to carry on his own dark musings there, 'this appearance was no more, but I found myself sitting on a pleasant bank beside a river by moon light hearing a harper who sung to the harp, and his theme was, The Man who never alters his opinion is like standing water, and breeds reptiles of the mind' (E 41). The Leviathan thus turns out to be a *paper monster* or a *paper tiger* (note that Leviathan's 'forehead was divided into streaks of green and purple like those on a tigers forehead ...', E 40). And the *persona* can deduct his own subtle metaphysical (Swedenborgian) lesson from what he has seen: 'All that we saw was owing to your metaphysics: for when you ran away, I found myself on a bank by moonlight hearing a harper ...' (E 41).[45] The Angel in this perspective represents exactly the kind of 'spectatorial subject-positioning' stressed by the UEA English Studies Group in their paper on the debate on the French Revolution in England - a debate that most certainly 'breeds *reptiles of the mind*' in those who take part in it! It is precisely because they cannot *touch* what they (can only) *see* that the participants in this debate are bound to *monsterize* their findings over and over again!

3. The French Revolution

The Marriage of Heaven and Hell may be read as a kind of metacommentary on the French Revolution. But Blake is concerned with the revolutionary issue in many other texts written during the last decade of the eighteenth century. In *The French Revolution* (1791) Blake describes in a series of apocalyptic images the initial events of the revolution in France, focusing in particular on the confrontation between the National Assembly ('the Senate') and the forces of the *ancien régime* (the King and his satellites). In *America a Prophecy* (1793) Blake recapitulates the events of the American revolution and/or War of Independence, but 'reads' these historical signs in the light of more recent French experiences (see the reference near the end of *America* to France receiving 'the Demon's [i.e. Orc's] light' after an intervening twelve-year period during which 'Angels and weak men ... should govern o'er the strong', E 56).[46] And finally, *The Book of Ahania* (1795) may be read as a mythopoetic rendering of some of the decisive events leading up to the Terror and to Thermidor in France - a portrayal of some of the self-destructive, pseudo-oedipal struggles of the early 1790's and the 'final' outcome of that *débâcle*.[47] What is interesting in this connection, however, is that these three texts by Blake may be said to reflect what Lynn Hunt has called 'the transformation of narrative structures that informed revolutionary rhetoric'.[48] *The French Revolution* is still dominated by 'the "generic plot" of comedy', whereas *America* marks a shift from comedy to romance ('Now the Revolution seemed more like a quest, in which the heroes were the brothers of the revolutionary fraternity, who faced a series of life-and-death struggles with the demonic forces of counterrevolution').[49] And in *The Book of Ahania* - written *after* Thermidor - the rhetoric of the last months of the 'radical' phase of the French Revolution seems to overdetermine the 'tragic' diction of the prophetic poem:

> In tragedy, the half-human, half-divine hero (in France, the increasingly isolated republican leadership) has had an extraordinary destiny almost within his grasp, and the glory of his efforts never quite fades. The tragedy is that the goal was so right, yet the quest for it inevitably failed.[50]

From the very outset the imagery of *The French Revolution* focuses on what Lynn Hunt, summarizing 'the generic plot' of comedy terms 'a conflict between an older social order ... and a new one'[51] or on what Stephen Prickett sees as 'a conflict between youth and age, sickness and health', where 'the cycles of natural decay and regeneration are couched in apocalyptic and prophetic language'.[52] This perspective on the revolution - emphasizing the 'final *reconciliation*, the happy emergence of the new society' - was characteristic of the early phase of the French Revolution.[53] The Revolu-tion was 'read' as a story with a happy ending. In Blake's *The French Revolution* this ethos informs the text insofar as the poem attempts to bring about a reconciliation between its antagonistic 'orders' or classes. The two principal characters Blake has given this role as mediators between different class positions are Sieyès and the Duke of Orléans - representing the clergy and the nobility respectively, but simultaneously transcending the narrowly defined ideological positions of the orders to which they belong.

The Abbé Sieyès thus envisages a future society where the class egoism of the old feudal classes (clergy and nobility) has become a thing of the past:

> Then the valleys of France shall cry to the soldier, 'throw down thy sword and musket,
> And run and embrace the meek peasant'. Her Nobles shall hear and shall weep, and put off
> The red robe of terror, the crown of oppression, the shoes of contempt, and unbuckle
> The girdle of war from the desolate earth; then the Priest in his thund'rous cloud
> Shall weep, bending to earth embracing the valleys, and putting his hand to the plow,
> Shall say, 'No more I curse thee; but now I will bless thee: No more in deadly black
> Devour thy labour; nor lift up a cloud in thy heavens, O laborious plough ...'
>
> (E 292)

Actually, the Priest's prophetic speech goes on for several more lines (we must remember that it is a speech-within-a-speech insofar as it is quoted in extenso by his colleague, the Abbé Sieyès). What 'the Priest' envisages in his speech, however, is the abolition of old class barriers (the class barriers of feudal society) and in particular the collapse of the distinction between *manual* and *mental* labour (the Priest 'puts his hand' to the plow).[54] The Priest is furthermore associated with a 'thund'rous cloud' - a symbol with inherently antagonistic connotations insofar as it may be associated with revolutionary *fire* as well as reactionary *opacity* (cf. later on in *The French Revolution* the reference to a peasant over whose head 'the soul of Voltaire shone *fiery*', while 'over the army Rousseau his white *cloud* / Unfolded ...', E 295, my italics)! In the future society celebrated by the Priest there is no need for the *miles Christianus* either - nor for the kind of militaristic terrorism on which the old feudal classes have based their power (see the reference to 'the *red robe of terror*'). Orléans in his speech likewise presents a vision of an 'organic' society, a 'body politic', where the many-sided development of one individual or class no longer obstructs or makes impossible the many-sided development of other individuals or classes, for '... can Nobles be bound when the people are free, or God weep when his children are happy?' (E 291).

We notice that in the Abbé Sieyès' speech it is a character who speaks on behalf of the revolution and its radical ideas that occupies 'the linguistic high ground, taking over the language of the Bible and of nature for his case' (cf. Prickett on Burke). The solemn use of the Biblical 'shall' (a 'prophetic' future tense) is just one of the stylistic 'markers' that points in the direction of such a type of rhetoricity (cf. also the use of parallelisms, the oblique reference to the Epistle to the Ephesians and 'the whole armour of God', 'the breastplate of righteousness', 'the shield of faith', etc. (6,13-16), the allegorical and 'metonymical' images, etc., etc.). What Blake stages is thus a 'putting-into-discourse' of the revolution where the oppressed classes - or rather their speakers, i.e. those who speak *on their behalf*, but who are at the same time distanced from them - adopt the ceremonial forms and the rhetorical codes mastered by the oppressing class in order to turn them to different and diametrically opposed purposes. The distancing devices of the linguistic and rhetorical codes of the ruling classes are here transformed into a means of approaching subjects (speakers) to each other (what is 'high' here literally 'bends' to what is 'low', thus 'de-constructing' the violent hierarchy that Derrida refers to in the passage quoted above, stressing as it were the *tactile* potentials inherent in language).[55]

The problem raised by the text - and of course, in a sense this is the problem of any revolutionary discourse - may be termed the problem of *representativity*. Who represents whom? Who speaks on behalf of whom? The UEA English Studies Group refers to 'a certain failure to unify a multiplicity of discourses' and to '... the crisis of representation of which the French Revolution is the first modern manifestation: who or what speaks in history? who speaks to interpret history? and on whose behalf?'.[56] Blake's text - like Price's (see above) - focuses on *the human voice*, on *elocutionary power*. The 'linguistic high ground' of the poem becomes the site of a rhetorical contest, a verbal *agon* or 'flyting', and in this contest power over language must be wrested from the opponent. This joust has also got certain oedipal overtones, and insofar as it is a struggle between the old and the new its terms are (so to speak) comprised by 'the "generic plot" of comedy' - and according to the narrative logic of this mode the new society is bound to win the contest. In the last resort the old feudal classes (the King and his council) represent not only a senescent and moribund patriarchy (from his window the King sees 'the old mountains of France, like aging men, fading away', and he is trying with his followers to awake 'from slumbers of five thousand years ...', E 283) - the old classes represent the forces of *death* in their life-and-death struggle with 'the Commons' and their supporters. This becomes clear in the very opening lines of *The French Revolution*:

The dead brood over Europe, the cloud and vision descends over chearful France;
O cloud well appointed! Sick, sick: the Prince on his couch, wreath'd in dim
And appalling mist; his strong hand outstretch'd, from his shoulder down the bone
Runs aching cold into the scepter too heavy for mortal grasp ...

(E 282-83)

This opening passage may be read as a poetic rendering of Thomas Paine's denunciation of Burke's traditionalism and view of England as an 'organic' society in his *Reflections on the Revolution in France*; Burke's argument is (in Paine's paraphrase) that the parliament of 1688 (the year of the Glorious Revolution) has attempted to 'bind all posterity for ever'. Paine is on posterity's side:

> I am contending for the rights of the *living*, and against their being willed away, and controlled and contracted for, by the manuscript assumed authority of the dead; and Mr Burke is contending for the authority of the dead over the rights and freedom of the living.[57]

In Blake's phrase 'The dead brood over Europe ...', and their ghostly presence is intended to prolong this state of affairs ('the authority of the dead over the rights and freedom of the living') *indefinitely*. The 'Gothic' atmosphere of *The French Revolution*, its constant references to dreams and omens and apparitions, etc., and the reiterated attempts on the part of the representatives of the old regime to 'monsterize' their opponents (the Council envisaging 'monsters of worlds unknown' swimming round them, 'watching to be delivered', E 289) - all these features point in the same direction. What all these signs and portents suggest or hint at is the phantasmatic or phantasmagoric event signalized by Michel de Certeau as 'the death of the father', and the imagery of Blake's poem bears witness to this specific Enlightenment or post-Enlightenment plight:

> The 'father' does not die. His 'death' is only another legend and his law remains. Everything takes place as if it were forever impossible to kill this deceased father, and as if 'taking account' of him ... just meant that he is simply displaced once more, and that he is precisely where we do not yet suspect his presence, in this self-same knowledge [i.e. a modern, secular, demystified knowledge belonging to a disenchanted world] and in the 'profit' this knowledge seems to ascertain.[58]

The Archbishop of Paris envisages this ghostly paternal presence as 'An aged form, white as snow, hov'ring in the mist ...' (E 288) and goes on at some length to elaborate on the 'significance' of this oneiric phantasm. All these ghostly signifiers are constantly evoked in the speeches of the representatives of the *ancien régime*, and they seem to point to an attempt on the part of these conservative speakers to 'ground' or anchor the signifying chains of their rhetorical performance. The 'noble' diction of these speeches (by the Archbishop of Paris, by the Duke of Burgundy, *et al.*)[59] marks the speakers as being linked up with the type of 'public sphere' that Habermas has termed *repräsentative Öffentlichkeit* and which is characterized by a specific 'aura' as well as by a strongly codified behaviour and appearance, by the symbolic use of 'ensigns' and a special body-language, and by a specific type of *rhetoric*.[60] *The French Revolution* portrays the (gradual) decay and breakdown of this symbolic apparatus - the 'aura' surounding the King - leading inevitably to the heat death of the feudal cosmos: the 'aching cold' running down 'into the scepter' at the beginning of the text gradually spreads out and becomes an all-pervasive force at the end of the poem, indicating that for the old classes the clock has run down (cf. the tragedy of kingship in Shakespeare's *Macbeth* or *King Lear*):[61]

> Pale and cold sat the King in midst of his peers, and his noble heart sunk, and his pulses
> Suspended their motion, a darkness crept over his eye-lids, and chill cold sweat
> Sat round his brows faded in faint death ...
> ...
>   ... The cold newt
> And snake, and damp toad, on the kingly foot crawl, or croak on the awful knee,
> Shedding their slime ...
>
>   (E 295-296)

According to Karl Marx in his *Kritik des Hegelschen Staatsrechts* (1843) the 'zoological point of view' ('*zoologische* Anschauungsweise') is characteristic of the nobility and 'finds in heraldry its corresponding branch of knowledge', for 'the secret of the nobility is *zoology*'.[62] *The French Revolution* marks the breakdown of this codified symbolism, insofar as the nobility (and the monarch) in the final *tableau* seem incapable of maintaining a distance to the animal kingdom - the lowly creatures invading the royal chambers as a corporeal presence are no longer envisaged as 'emblematic' expressions of a self-conscious caste; they bring about a 'monsterizing' of the very class itself whose deepest fears turned on (and were turned on by) the phantasms of a 'monstrous' revolution.[63]

At this point in the text the rhetoric of the old feudal classes has been *silenced*. The stratified, 'hierarchical' language of the *ancien régime* has been supplanted by a different idiom - 'the voice of the people, arising from valley and hill, / O'erclouded with power' (E 292). In accordance with the rhetoric of the sublime what has taken place may be termed a 'transference of power' from one speaking subject to another (Neil Hertz).[64] But the question is if this 'transference of power' has effectively taken place. For at the end of *The French Revolution* 'the voice of the people' seems to be silenced as well. Instead, Blake visualizes 'the Senate' (i.e. the National Assembly) sitting 'in peace, beneath morning's beam' (E 296), i.e. what Blake stages here is another *tableau* or a purely iconographic representation of what Starobinski has called 'the solar myth' of the French Revolution.[65]

Instead of an exchange of words - and a transference of rhetorical power - we are presented with a transference of light: *le roi soleil* has been superseded by a more popular and a more 'democratic' version of 'morning's beam'. And the spectacle recalls the extensive use of light symbolism in a number of texts commenting on the French Revolution (cf. also Price's reference to 'the light you have struck out ... reflected to FRANCE, and there kindled into a blaze that lays despotism in ashes ...'). In Thomas Paine's words, 'There is a *morning of reason* rising upon man on the subject of government, that has not appeared before ...'.[66] In a sense this may be regarded as the fulfilment of the En*light*enment project. But in another sense the 'name of the father' - to use a Lacanian term - is still hovering in the air, for the revolutionaries have not been able to free themselves from the linguistic codes and norms of their opponents, i.e. from the language of a *hierarchical* society. Only an *apocalyptic* language seems capable of 'containing' all these conflicting voices - voices referring to other voices referring to other voices, etc., *ad libitum* and *ad infinitum*. In all this turmoil, in this cacophany of voices there is no transcendental subject (cf. Derrida's reference to John in *The Book of Revelation* as transmitting a message 'already transmitted', in a text containing 'so many sendings, *envois*, so many voices, and this puts so many people on the telephone line')![67] But in this rhetorical *bricolage* the 'father' cannot be killed off either - he lives on *in language*. As 'the graves of arch-angels [are] unseal'd' at the end of *The French Revolution* we witness a turbulent reanimation of *all* the signifying chains, a violent return to the absent *origin* (E 296).

4. *America a Prophecy*

In *The French Revolution* sexuality seems to play only a peripheral role, and femininity and female values are similarly marginalized in the text; there is a reference to the love life of 'the wild raging millions' (E 292), allegedly undergoing a refinement, insofar as the males are envisaged as wooing their 'once savage loves, now beaming with knowledge, with gentle awe adorned ...' (E 293), but this 'civilizing' of eroticism seems to be only a parenthesis in the revolutionary process. What is emphasized in *The French Revolution* is republican virtue, and this virtue is clearly associated with a *heroic masculinity* (cf. the way revolutionary leaders and sympathizers such as Sieyès, Orléans, Fayette, etc., are portrayed). In *America* (1793), however, sexuality and politics are interwoven to such an extent that it is virtually impossible to separate them from each other. This prophecy was written at a time when the French revolution was going through its most radical stages, and it therefore is not surprising that we find in this prophecy traces of what Lynn Hunt identifies as the generic plot of *romance*: 'Now the Revolution seemed more like a quest, in which the heroes were the brothers of the revolutionary fraternity, who faced a series of life-and-death struggles with the demonic forces of counterrevolution'.[68] This is the archetypal situation presented at the beginning of Blake's prophecy:

> The guardian Prince of Albion burns in his nightly tent,
> Sullen fires across the Atlantic glow to America's shore:
> Piercing the souls of warlike men, who rise in silent night,
> Washington, Franklin, Paine & Warren, Gates, Hancock & Green ...

(E 51)

The heroes of the American War of Independence are portrayed as 'the brothers of [a] revolutionary fraternity', banded together against and confronting their demonic adversary, 'The Guardian Prince of Albion', i.e. the English King; later 'Albions wrathful Prince' is envisaged as a mythical 'dragon form clashing his scales at midnight' (E 51). Thus the heroes are from the very outset presented as heroic dragon-slayers. According to Northrop Frye, 'the hero of romance is analogous to the mythical Messiah or deliverer who comes from an upper world, and his enemy is analogous to the demonic powers of a lower world'.[69] And 'The central form of quest-romance is the *dragon-killing* theme exemplified in the stories of St. George and Perseus ...'.[70] Furthermore, 'the reward of the quest is usually or includes a bride ...', and she 'is often to be found in a perilous, forbidden, or tabooed place'.[71] All these literary motifs appear in a more or less modified form in Blake's *America*. The revolutionary leaders are attempting a head-on attack on the dragon of royal power or monarchical tyranny (George III), but at the same time the archetypal rebel Orc is 'serpent-form'd' (E 52) and therefore does not belong whole-heartedly or univocally to the 'upper world' (the realm of light), but in a sense also to a demonic underworld or anti-world. *America* furthermore refers to a bride 'to be found in a perilous, forbidden, or tabooed place' (Frye), insofar as Blake explores the Atlantis myth, presenting us with a visionary panorama of the Atlantic Ocean transformed into its opposite, a 'Golden World', where 'An ancient palace, archetype of mighty Emperies, / Rears its immortal pinnacles, built in the forest of God / by Ariston the king of beauty *for his stolen bride*' (E 54, my italics). The prize of the contest thus turns out to be *a damsel in distress* - but on the other hand the 'legitimacy' of the heroes' enterprise is called in question, insofar as their 'precursor' (Ariston) seems to have abducted his bride or taken her from a rival.[72] The sexual motif is touched upon again, however, when the repercussions of the American revolution in England are detailed in visionary terms by Blake and he refers to the liberation of sexual desire as one of the effects of the revolutionary process, 'Leaving the females naked and glowing with the lusts of youth' (E 56). *The fires of Orc* are destructive not only of political stability - this is what the *architectural* metaphors intimate[73] - but also of any kind of law-and-order policy in the realm of sexuality, for 'The doors of marriage are open, and the Priests in rustling scales / Rush into reptile coverts ...' (E 56).

In the 'Preludium' to *America a Prophecy* Blake offers a shorthand 'summary' of the political conflict that he describes at some length in the prophecy proper, and in the 'Preludium' he translates the selfsame conflict (the American colonies' struggle for freedom in the War of Independence) into a *sexual myth* (or to put it in Freudian terms, a 'family romance'). America's 'coming of age' is envisaged as 'the hairy youth' Orc's arriving at the age of puberty and his subsequent initiation into sexuality, when he 'seizes' his gaoler's daughter in an attempt to liberate himself as well as her:

> The shadowy daughter of Urthona stood before red Orc.
> When fourteen suns had faintly journey'd o'er his dark abode;
> His food she brought in iron baskets, his drink in cups of iron;
> ...
> Silent as despairing love, and strong as jealousy,
> The hairy shoulders rend the links, free are the wrists of fire;
> Round the terrific loins he siez'd the panting struggling womb ...

> (E 50)

In his famous pamphlet *Common Sense* (1776) Thomas Paine had already thematized the political issue as a kind of 'youth revolution' (politics was frequently 'biologized' in the debate between loyalists and revolutionaries during that period),[74] for he stated that 'the general temper of the colonies, towards a British government, will be like that of a youth, who is *nearly out of his time*; they will care very little about her'.[75] In Blake's 'preludium' Paine's 'hardened, sullen tempered Pharao of [England]'[76] has been replaced by the mythical figure *Urthona*, representing in this context the *earth-owners* of England, i.e. the British oligarchy.[77] Insofar as Urthona in other Blakean (con)texts is synonymous with Los (the artist-hero) and Los is Orc's father, it becomes clear that Orc's desire for the 'shadowy daughter of Urthona' is a desire for his own sister (the presence of this *incest* motif turns the narrative into a 'family romance'). The *displaced bride* of Blake's text (the prophetic poem) thus represents not only a reinterpretation of the symbolic terms of the debate on the American, and by implication, the

French, Revolution - focusing on the conflict between age and youth, and on the theme of 'maturity' in its Kantian sense[78] - but also a *sexualization* of the whole conflict and its terms. According to Michel Foucault, this *sexualization of politics* is characteristic of the bourgeois era as such,[79] and in the eighteenth century it might on some occasions be propounded in a fairly direct way as an 'ideological' attempt not only to redefine political power, but also to come to terms with economic 'potency'. This is the way it is presented, for instance, in a utopian scheme set forth in 1789 by two Swedes belonging to the Swedenborgian community in London in a pamphlet entitled *Plan for a free Community upon the Coast of Africa*:

> ... the first elementary, powerful, and universal Union, or Bond of Society, is the *Love of the Sex* ... Nothing ... is more true, than that the *Love of the Sex*, and the constant exercise thereof, which is the *Virile Potency*, is the very basis to the accession of all other kinds of *permanent Powers* ... It is ... evident why a Man with the permanent *Power of Virility*, stands on the sure foundation of being exalted to every *Power of Wealth* and *Dignity* ...[80]

Even if Wadström and Nordenskiöld are implicated in a *utopian* project, it is also clear that their 'bourgeois' utopianism is based on an instrumentalization of sexuality. Blake's emphasis on sexuality in *America* is drawing attention to something else - to the 'dark' aspects of the revolutionary romance. The forces of counterrevolution cannot be conquered once and for all, for the revolutionary 'brother horde' seems to be just as 'serpent-form'd' as its mythical adversary. The metaphorics of light is replaced by the metaphorics of fire (cf. the references to 'the fires of Orc') - *burning down the house* (to quote Talking Heads) seems to be the final outcome of the revolutionary struggle, the only way to overcome the 'law-built heaven' of institutionalized religion and institutionalized tyranny (E 56). But the problem with all these revolutionary signifiers is that it seems to be impossible to control them - to map out their 'legitimate' territories or determine the 'scope' of their implications. When and how do the 'sullen fires' (E 51) of despotism become transformed into their own antithesis in order to bring about a cathartic upheaval, a universal conflagration?

As an example of the way revolutionary discourse appropriates the 'generic plot' of romance in order to interpret historical events one might take the 'ADDRESS of the FRENCH NATION to the COMBINED POWERS', written by Robespierre and later published by Daniel Eaton in an English translation in his *Politics for the People: or, A Salmagundy for Swine* (Part II, Number I, 1794); this text was presented to the National Convention on December 5th 1793. Robespierre's rhetorical strategy is in accordance with Lynn Hunt's characterization of romance: '... on the one side are the almost mythical heroes, and on the other are the villains, the cowards, the dragons'.[81] In Robespierre's words the National Convention can show 'to the friends and enemies of France honourable scars and glorious mutilations', and 'The whole Convention braves death and the fury of all tyrants'.[82] These tyrants and their allies, on the other hand, are portrayed in animalistic terms as belonging to a demonized anti-world: 'The world was the exclusive property of two or three races of tyrants, as the desert wilds of Africa are the domains of *tigers and serpents*. We have restored it to mankind ...'.[83] The quarrel turns out to be a quarrel about *signifiers* - who has the right to 'use' or interpret the 'master-signifiers' of Western culture? What is disputed here seems to be *the question of hermeneutical power*. In Robespierre's perspective the authority that 'guarantees' the authenticity of the historical mission of the revolutionaries is 'the Supreme Being': 'What people ever offered so pure a worship of the Supreme Being as we do?'.[84] But are the revolutionaries actually capable of defending 'the linguistic high ground' that they have (temporarily?) occupied? Have they 'stolen' their signifiers just as Ariston had 'stolen' his bride? What can be achieved by means of these usurped heroic avatars?

In the parodic 'The Life, Death, and Wonderful Atchievements of Edmund Burke. A new Ballad', written by 'the Author of the Wrongs of Africa' (1792), the generic plot of romance is exploited for satirical purposes and Burke himself turned into a quixotic scribbler, a knight-errant of tropes and figures:

> Reasons like red hot balls he threw,
> With Edmund none could cope;
> But in a metaphor was slain,
> Or perish'd by a trope.[85]

Slain in a metaphor or *perished by a trope*! This is the way the revolution ends - not with a bang, but with verbal mud-slinging. The revolutionary struggle is turned into *a battle of books*!

W.J.T. Mitchell has shown how Blake uses the interplay between text and illustrations in his illuminated books to create 'a kind of counterpoint in which each medium proceeds with its own independent formal integrity, while interacting with the other to form a complex, unified whole'.[86] In *America* Blake thus 'shows' us Orc when the text refers to the repressive and tyrannous 'Urizen' and vice versa.[87] In this way Blake manages to point out the relativity of the antithetical 'positions' represented by the two figures respectively - and this relativization further contributes to the destabilization of the master-signifiers of revolutionary as well as counter-revolutionary rhetoric. This textual strategy might be said to effect *a 'deconstructive' turn*.

5. *The Book of Ahania*

In *The Book of Ahania* (1795) the signifiers of revolutionary discourse are undergoing a further de-construction. In this prophecy it might be said that 'an undercurrent of the third generic plot', i.e. that of tragedy, comes 'to the surface' (to quote Lynn Hunt).[88] On the other hand, in *The Book of Ahania* Blake has made it much more difficult to recognize the historical agents in the revolutionary - and post-revolutionary - drama the text unfolds. These historical agents tend to disappear altogether behind *the mythical narrative* of the text. But behind the father-son conflict set forth by the prophetic poem one may discern the historical clash between the old feudal classes and the revolutionary masses (or the *revolutionary leadership*):

> Fuzon, on a chariot iron-wing'd
> On spiked flames rose; his hot visage
> Flam'd furious! Sparkles his hair & beard
> Shot down his wide bosom and shoulders.
> On clouds of smoke rages his chariot
> And his right hand burns red in its cloud
> Moulding into a vast globe, his wrath
> As the thunder-stone is moulded.
> Son of Urizens silent burnings

(E 83)

The struggle between Fuzon and Urizen (son and father) has replaced the struggle between Orc and Urthona (or Orc and Urizen) in *America*; in *The Book of Ahania* this struggle is even more overtly oedipal than in the former prophecy (Fuzon is '*Son* of Urizens silent burnings'). The sublimity of the revolutionary project is intimated through the metaphorical reference to thunder-and-lightning (cf. Longinus on the way in which 'a well-timed flash of sublimity scatters everything before it like a bolt of lightning and reveals the full power of the speaker at a single stroke ...').[89] But the sublime of the revolution is opposed by the counter-sublime of 'Urizens silent burnings' - and it furthermore turns out that Urizen has it in his power to 'monsterize' the whole project of his opponent(s) by using the poisonous blood of 'an enormous dread Serpent' (E 84) as a deadly weapon (he poisons a *rock* and hurls it at Fuzon). The rock actually kills Fuzon - or so it seems, for afterwards the 'corse' seems to come alive again, even after Urizen has crucified it 'On the accursed Tree of MYSTERY' (E 86):

> ... Forth flew the arrows of pestilence
> Round the pale living Corse on the tree

(E 86)

Fuzon's *imitatio Christi* (and his death) cannot be certified - he keeps 'groaning' on the Tree (E 87). But Fuzon's death on the other hand clearly mirrors the tragic outcome of the revolutionary process in the fatal Year II ('The tragedy is that the goal was so right, yet the quest for it inevitably failed. The heroes who nevertheless made the attempt were making a noble sacrifice of themselves for the sake of the community ...').[90] In the last months of his life Robespierre in his speeches 'sounded many tragic notes in the midst of continuing themes of romance'.[91] Fuzon's death mirrors that of his revolutionary colleague Robespierre, insofar as he like the latter seems to be guilty of *hubris*, 'unloosing' the tigers of wrath ('those French Tigers')[92] allegedly to subvert his opponent's autocratic regime but at the same time 'usurping' his very position:

... While Fuzon his tygers unloosing
Thought Urizen slain by his wrath.
I am God. said he, eldest of things!

(E 85)

In this connection we may recall that after Ninth Thermidor Robespierre was accused of having tried to appropriate to himself a godlike status, a 'divinity' that he was far from possessing in the eyes of his opponents. Thus Thuriot in the National Convention refers to 'this man who was so small, yet wanted to be so great, and who if he had only been able to do it would have dethroned the Eternal Being in order to put himself in His place ...'.[93]

Fuzon does not know where he is inserted into the symbolic order - in this sense 'the father cannot die', to quote Michel de Certeau, for Fuzon only attempts to kill his father in order to become like him, to 'rematerialize' him. As far as this compulsive pattern is concerned, he is dominated by *a metaphysical quest for 'the first', for priority* ('I am God. said he, *eldest* of things!').[94] The futility of such a search for origins, for primacy, has been pointed out by poststructuralists for the last two decades - in this sense Blake is in accordance with the 'deconstructive' turn of philosophy with (and after) Derrida!

In *The Book of Ahania* the rock that Urizen hurls at Fuzon is subsequently metamorphosed into 'Mount Sinai, in Arabia' (E 85), i.e. into the mountain where Moses received the tablets of the law. Later Fuzon is crucified on 'the topmost stem' of the Tree of Mystery, growing on top of another rock-mountain, and here it may be recalled that at the Festival of the Supreme Being an artificial mountain had been constructed, representing according to Carol Blum 'the Jacobin movement'; Robespierre himself had celebrated the 'Love of mountains' as 'the mark of the superior soul', referring in the Prospectus of the *Défenseur de la Constitution* to his new position as 'having descended from the rostrum of the French senate' to 'climb to the rostrum of the universe'.[95] At the same time Robespierre's own role at the festival of the Supreme Being - taking place just a few weeks before his fall - also seemed to stress the tragic and 'sacrificial' aspects of his position, for (according to Carol Blum) he was on that occasion wearing a 'Werther costume', insofar as his yellow pants and blue jacket 'carried the connotations of the "suicide costume", and Robespierre's presentation of his public person attired in this widely understood sign of impending sacrifice carried the message that the Terrorist was to be known as his own victim'.[96] This is pretty close to what is happening in *The Book of Ahania*: here Fuzon is crucified in the middle of an elevated, but 'denaturalized' landscape, where human and vegetable forms intermingle and the letter of the law (Urizen's 'book of iron', E 85) dominates the scene. The revolutionary 'figure' is thus re-inscribed *in the canonical book!*[97] It turns out to be impossible for the revolutionary to get rid of the (name of the) father - the representative of the law whose very function the rebel-son tries to take possession of.

6. The Mythos of Winter

After Thermidor the rhetoric of revolutionary (and counter-revolutionary) discourse seems to enter a fourth phase - after having by turns exploited the generic plot of comedy, romance, and tragedy. According to Friedrich Schlegel (writing in 1798) the French Revolution may be regarded as 'die furchbarste *Groteske* des Zeitalters'.[98] Ronald Paulson in his *Representations of Revolution (1789-1820)* refers to contemporary artists 'producing monsters in the grotesque sense of doubles or figures possessed by other figures' and discerns an epistemological trend towards 'undifferentiation' as characteristic of post-Thermidorian Europe (a trend to be found in some cases even before the Terror and before Thermidor): 'Undifferentiation is a characteristic shared by the gothic and the grotesque ... both gothic and grotesque focus on the moment of estrangement, the transition between this world and that [i.e. our normal world and a 'demonic' world], when plant and human are in metamorphosis in the process of growing indistinguishable'.[99] In Northrop Frye's perspective we might interpret the fourth scenario - that of the Revolution as 'die furchtbarste Groteske des Zeitalters' - as the 'generic plot' of what Frye calls irony and satire; here we are concerned with 'the mythical patterns of experience, the attempts to give form to the shifting ambiguities and complexities of unidealized existence'.[100] In terms of Frye's seasonal symbolism what we find in irony and satire is *the mythos of winter*, and the wheel has thus come full circle, insofar as the three other 'modes' that Lynn Hunt focused on in her reading of revolutionary rhetoric, i.e. comedy, romance, and tragedy, were linked to spring, summer, and autumn respectively. By means of a circuitous *détour* the French Revolution seems to have *deconstructed* itself - returning in the end to square one, as it were.

In Blake's reading(s) of the French Revolution the bias towards the fourth scenario (that of irony and satire, or that of the grotesque) seems to have been there all the time, however. The way in which his *Marriage of Heaven and Hell* tends to deconstruct its own images and undermine their symbolic import has already been mentioned. In *The French Revolution* it is also possible to discern a similar trend, insofar as the rhetorical efforts of the speakers gradually seem to be taken over by and incorporated into an entropic state of undifferentiation, where the King and his satellites more and more tend to become statuesque fixtures in a totally immobilized setting. Whereas Blake in his *Marriage* seemed to celebrate the way(s) in which 'hierarchical' differences (between high and low, angel and devil, etc.) might be destroyed in the acid bath of a revolutionary *écriture*, he later became much more pessimistic with regard to the ultimate effects of 'printing in the infernal method, by corrosives, which in Hell are medicinal and salutary ...' (E 38). In one of his last letters (to George Cumberland, dated 12 April 1827) he expresses his post-revolutionary disillusionment in the following way, linking it up with his preference for the *firm outline*:

> For a Line or Lineament is not formed by Chance a Line ... is Itself & Not Intermeasurable with or by any Thing Else Such is Job but since the French Revolution Englishmen are all Intermeasurable One by Another Certainly a happy state of Agreement to which I for One do not Agree.
>
> (E 707)

In England the spectacle of the French Revolution thus seems to have resulted only in a social and political levelling process comprising all and sundry - it has apparently given rise to a society where one individual is interchangeable with another. The fear of the French example - the anxiety provoked by the revolutionaries as 'the carriers of desire' - had disrupted and destabilized the very self-image of the English public, making them withdraw into a kind of anonymous collectivity (comparable to the Heideggerian 'das Man'). Vis-à-vis this great disenchantment, however, Blake remains faithful to his symbolic role as artist-rebel (Los) - Los who goes on building the golden city of human hope (Golgonooza) in spite of the alienating consequences of the industrial revolution, while the latter brings forth a civilization of 'intricate wheels ..., wheel without wheel: / To perplex youth in their outgoings, and to bind to labours in Albion / Of day

& night the myriads of eternity ...' (*Jerusalem*, plate 65, E 214). In this brave new world the worker is just a cog in a huge and complicated machinery. But the revolution as a cosmic process and project - and as a consciousness-raising undertaking - remains to Blake a constant task and concern, even if it may be 'the labour of ages' to create just 'a little flower' (E 37).

Notes

The references to Blake are to *The Poetry and Prose of William Blake*, edited by David V. Erdman, commentary by Harold Bloom (Garden City, New York, Doubleday: fourth printing, with revisions, 1970). (E).

1. Stephen Prickett, *England and the French Revolution* (Houndmills, Basingstoke, Hampshire: Macmillan Education Ltd., 1989), pp. 12-13.
2. Ibid., p. 13.
3. Ibid., p. 13.
4. Olivia Smith, *The Politics of Language 1791-1819* (Oxford: Clarendon Press, 1984, 1986), p. 74.
5. Edmund Burke, *Reflections on the Revolution in France* (Harmondsworth, Middlesex: Penguin Books, reprinted 1973), p. 140 ('The temple of honour ought to be seated on an eminence ...').
6. Olivia Smith, op. cit., p. 76.
7. E.P. Thompson, *The Making of the English Working Class* (Harmondsworth, Middlesex: Penguin Books, reprinted 1972), p. 55.
8. William Hamilton Reid, *The Rise and Dissolution of the Infidel Societies in this Metropolis* (London, 1800), p. 91 (Reid's italics).
9. Ibid., p. 92 (Reid's italics). On the dissenting tradition and on millenarian movements in England and France in the period of the French Revolution cf. also Clarke Garrett, *Respectable Folly. Millenarians and the French Revolution in France and England* (Baltimore & London: The John Hopkins University Press, 1975).
10. William Reid, op.cit., p. 2. Reid refers to the 'prophetic' activities of Richard Brothers, 'the Prince of the Hebrews' or 'the Great Prophet of Paddington Street' (1757-1824).
11. E.P. Thompson, op.cit., p. 56.
12. Richard Price, *A Discourse of the Love of Our Country*, Sixth Edition, with Additions (London, 1790), pp. 49-50.
13. Lynn Hunt, *Politics, Culture, and Class in the French Revolution* (London: Methuen & Co. Ltd., 1984), pp. 34-35.
14. Edmund Burke, op.cit., p. 194. Burke obviously alludes to the medieval legend describing the magical feats of 'Virgilius' (i.e. Virgil). Cf. *Early English Prose Romances*, ed. William J. Thoms, Vol. II (London, 1858), pp. 56-58. Virgil makes his servant cut him 'in peces' (p. 56) in order to be rejuvenated, but because of the Emperor's intervention the magical 'cure' miscarries, and Virgil remains *dead* in the end!

15. Sigmund Freud, 'The "Uncanny"', *The Pelican Freud Library*, Vol. 14 (Harmondworth, Middlesex: Penguin Books, 1985), p. 362.
16. Sigmund Freud, *Totem and Taboo* (London: Routledge & Kegan Paul, 1960), p. 142.
17. Ronald Paulson, *Representations of Revolution (1789-1820)* (New Haven and London: Yale University Press, 1983), p. 89.
18. John Milton, *Paradise Lost*, Book I, lines 323-25, in *The Complete Poems* (London, Melbourne, Toronto, Dutton, New York: Dent, 1980), p. 166 (my italics).
19. Lynn Hunt, op. cit., p. 37.
20. Ibid., p. 37.
21. Harold Bloom, 'Dialectic in The Marriage of Heaven and Hell' (1958), reprinted in *English Romantic Poets. Modern Essays in Criticism*, edited by M.H. Abrams (New York, Oxford: A Galaxy Book, Oxford University Press, 1960), p. 76. In *Anatomy of Criticism* (New York: Atheneum, 1966) Northrop Frye suggests that we should use the word 'anatomy' as a convenient name 'to replace the cumbersome and in modern times rather misleading "Menippean satire"' (p. 312). Lynn Hunt also uses some of the categories in *Anatomy of Criticism* as an analytical tool in her discussion of the 'poetics' of revolutionary discourse (Frye's 'theory of myths').
22. Mikhail Bakhtin, *Problems of Dostojevsky's Poetics* (Minneapolis: University of Minnesota Press, Second printing, 1985), p. 115, pp. 116-17.
23. Ibid., p. 114 (Bakhtin's italics).
24. Walter Benjamin, *Illuminations* (London: Collins/Fontana Books, 1973), p. 174.
25. Cf. Jacques Derrida, *Of Grammatology*. Translated by Gayatri Chakravorty Spivak, 'Translator's Preface' (Baltimore and London: The Johns Hopkins University Press, Fourth printing, 1980), p. lxxvi.
26. Mikhail Bakhtin, op. cit., p. 116.
27. Northrop Frye, op. cit., p. 163.
28. Ibid., p. 163.
29. Cf. Harold Bloom, op. cit., p. 77.
30. Cf. *Oeuvres de Maximilien Robespierre*, Tôme IX, *Discours, Septembre 1792-27 Juillet 1793* (Presses Universitaires de France, 1978), 'Séance du 3 décembre 1792', p. 123 (my translation).
31. *Liberty and Property Preserved Against Republicans and Levellers*, Number II (1792), p. 6, p. 8.
32. Charles Pigott, *A Political Dictionary* (London, 1795), p. 67.
33. 'Selected Writings of Thomas Spence 1750-1814', in: *Essays in honour of William Galacher* (Humboldt-Universität zu Berlin, 1966), p. 316. In *The Oracle*, 3 December 1793, a 'humourous' account of 'THE ORIGIN OF JACOBINISM' started with a reference to the Fall of the Rebel Angels: 'The DEVIL was the *first Jacobin*, for which he was hurled neck and heels out of heaven ...'. Quoted from *Politics for the People*, Vol. 1 (1793-1794) (New York: Greenwood Reprint Corporation, 1968), p. 173.
34. Jacques Derrida, *Positions* (Chicago and London: The University of Chicago Press, Phoenix edition, 1982), p. 41 (my italics).
35. See Charles Levin, 'La Greffe du Zèle: Derrida and the Cupidity of the Text', in: *The Structural Allegory. Reconstructive Encounters with the New French Thought*, edited by John Fekete (Manchester: Manchester University Press, 1984), p. 215.

36. See concerning these terms Mikhail Bakhtin, *Rabelais and His World* (Cambridge, Massachusetts, and London, England: The M.I.T. Press, 1968), pp. 368-436, and Freud's motto from Virgil's *Aeneid* in *The Interpretation of Dreams*: FLECTERE SI NEQUEO SUPEROS, ACHERONTA MOVEBO.
37. William Reid, op. cit., p. 113.
38. *The Works of the Right Honourable Edmund Burke*, Vol V (London, New York and Toronto: Oxford University Press, 1907), p. 266 (the first italics mine, whereas in the second instance they are Burke's italics).
39. *The Works and Correspondence of the Right Honourable Edmund Burke*, A New Edition, Vol V (London, 1852), p. 147 (my italics).
40. UEA English Studies Group (David Punter, David Aers, Robert Clark, Jonathan Cook, Thomas Elsasser), 'Strategies for Representing Revolution', in: *1789: Reading Writing Revolution*, ed. Francis Barker et al. (University of Essex, 1982), p. 86.
41. Ibid., p. 87.
42. Barbara Freeman, '*Frankenstein* with Kant: A Theory of Monstrosity, or the Monstrosity of Theory', *SubStance* No. 52 (1987), p. 22.
43. Martin K. Nurmi, *William Blake* (London: Hutchinson University Library, 1975), p. 82.
44. Quoted from *Political Verse and Song from Britain and Ireland*, edited by Mary Ashraf (London: Lawrence & Wishart, 1975), p. 96.
45. The formulation: 'this *appearance* was no more' contains an oblique reference to Swedenborg's doctrine of 'appearances' and offers a parodic version of the latter. Cf. Swedenborg's dogmatic statement: '... in the Spiritual World [animals] have an apparent Existence from the Affections of Angels and Spirits, so that they may be called the *Appearances* of their Affections; for which Reason also they immediately vanish, *as soon as ever the Angel or Spirit departs*, or his Affection ceases ...' ('Remarks on the Souls of Beasts', in: *Concerning the White Horse*, etc. (London, 1788), p. 72 (my italics)).
46. Concerning the 'twelve years' of wintry discontent see W.H. Stevenson's commentary in *The Poems of William Blake*, edited by W.H. Stevenson (London and New York: Longman, Norton, First paperback edition 1971), p. 205: 'The years from the American victory at Yorktown (1781) to the end of the rule of "weak men" with Louis XVI's execution in Jan. 1793 are probably meant'.
47. Cf. David V. Erdman, *Blake. Prophet Against Empire*, Revised Edition (New York: Anchor Books, Doubleday & Company, Garden City, 1969), pp. 314-15.
48. Lynn Hunt, op. cit., p. 34.
49. Ibid., p. 35.
50. Ibid., p. 37.
51. Ibid., p. 34.
52. Stephen Prickett, op. cit., p. 63. (Prickett's comment on *The French Revolution).*
53. Lynn Hunt, op. cit., pp. 34-35 (my italics).
54. Cf. Marx' comment on 'priestcraft' in *The German Ideology*: 'Division of labour only becomes truly such from the moment when a division of material and mental labour appears. (The first form of ideologists, *priests*, is concurrent.) ...'. *The German Ideology*, Part One (Lawrence & Wishart, London, reprinted 1985), p. 51. Sieyès is the author of the famous pamphlet *Qu'est que le Tiers état?* (1789), where he argues in favour of an abolition of feudal privileges: 'Il est sûr que la communauté des privilèges est le meilleur moyen *de rapprocher les ordres* et de

préparer la plus importante des lois, celle qui convertira les ordres en *une* nation' (first italics mine). (Emmanuel Sieyès: *Qu'est-ce que le Tiers état?*, Paris: Flammarion, 1988, p. 49, n. 2).

55. Whereas the King's relationship with the cosmic landscapes of the poem connotes mastery or an attempt to dominate these self-same landscapes (cf. 'The King lean'd on his mountains, then lifted his head and look'd on his armies, that shone / Through heaven, tinging morning beams with blood ...', E 287), what is thematized in the Abbé Sieyès' speech is rather a kind of 'homecoming', an *immediate* contact with the cosmos envisaged as a kind of Heideggerian 'Erde'.

56. UEA English Studies Group, op. cit., p. 85.

57. Thomas Paine, *Rights of Man* (Harmondsworth, Middlesex: Penguin Books, reprinted 1971), p. 64 (Paine's italics).

58. Michel de Certeau, *L'Écriture de l'histoire* (Paris: Gallimard, 1975), pp. 307-08 (my translation).

59. The Duke of Burgundy is (in actual fact) Louis the XVI's *dead* brother. According to Stephen Prickett, 'the dead brother had, in Daniel Eaton's words, given "early presage of excessive pride", and was therefore the perfect symbol of the diehard spirit of the French Crown' (Stephen Prickett, op. cit., p. 15). Cf. *Politics for the People*, op. cit., Vol. 1, p. 176: 'THE Duke of Burgundy ... felt all the importance of his being, his usual expression was, "God, the King, and myself".'

60. Cf. Jürgen Habermas, *Strukturwandel der Öffentlichkeit*, 5. Auflage als Sonderausgabe der Sammlung Luchterhand (Neuwied und Berlin: Luchterhand, 1971), pp. 20-21.

61. Cf. Ib Johansen, 'Narren og den gale. To renæssancefigurer', in: *Den jyske historiker*, nr. 26 (1983), pp. 33-37.

62. *MEW*, Band 1 (Berlin: Dietz Verlag, 1977), p. 311 (my translation).

63. Edmund Burke from the very outset made a monster of the Revolution, 'this *monstrous* tragi-comic scene', asserting emphatically: 'Everything seems out of nature in this strange chaos of levity and ferocity ...' (*Reflections on the Revolution in France*, op. cit., p. 92, my italics).

64. Cf. Neil Hertz' reading of Longinus on this topic in 'Lecture de Longin', *Poétique 15* (1973), p. 296, where he discusses 'the sublime turn' brought about by means of such a *transference of power*. By means of this 'sublime turn' the poetic subject takes possession of the very forces that threaten it.

65. Cf. Jean Starobinski, *1789. Les emblèmes de la raison* (Paris: Flammarion, 1979), pp. 31-37: 'Le mythe solaire de la révolution'. Starobinski refers to this (universal) metaphor as 'une image apollinienne, indéfiniment répétée' (p. 31).

66. Thomas Paine, op. cit., p. 230. Cf. p. 140: 'The revolutions of America and France have thrown a beam of light over the world, which reaches into man'.

67. Jacques Derrida, 'Of an Apocalyptic Tone Recently Adopted in Philosophy', *Semeia 23* (1982), p. 86.

68. Lynn Hunt, op. cit., p. 35

69. Northrop Frye, op. cit., p. 187.

70. Ibid., p. 189 (my italics).

71. Ibid., p. 193.

72. Concerning 'Ariston' (a mythical representative of an 'unfallen' nobility?) see Foster Damon, *A Blake Dictionary* (London: Thames and Hudson, 1973), p. 27. On the

Atlantis myth cf. also George Mills Harper, *The Neoplatonism of William Blake* (Chapel Hill: The University of North Carolina Press, 1961), pp. 219-27.

73. On 'The Architecture of the State' see Stephen Prickett, op. cit., pp. 158-71. On the one hand, architectural metaphors 'offered in a visible and concrete form the high abstract idea of the state as a human artifact ...', on the other they suggested that 'great buildings ... represented more than the rational planning of any one architect' (p. 158).

74. On the parent-child metaphor and its strategic implications in this debate see Edwin G. Burrows and Michael Wallace, 'The American Revolution: The Ideology and Psychology of National Liberation', in *Perspectives in American History*, Vol. VI (1972). The moot point was: *Had* America 'come of age'?

75. *The Thomas Paine Reader* (Harmondsworth, Middlesex: Penguin Books, 1987), p. 89 (my italics).

76. Ibid., p. 87.

77. Cf. on Blakean uses of etymology F.E. Pierce: 'Etymology as Explanation in Blake', *PQ*, X (1931). Foster Damon, however, just interprets *Urthona* as 'earth owner' (*A Blake Dictionary*, op. cit., p. 426).

78. Cf. Kant in: 'An Answer to the Question: "What is Enlightenment?"', in: *Kant's Political Writings* (Cambridge: Cambridge University Press, 1970), p. 54: *'Enlightenment is man's emergence from his self-incurred immaturity. Immaturity is the inability to use one's own understanding without the guidance of another ...'*.

79. Cf. Michel Foucault, *The History of Sexuality. Vol. I: An Introduction* (New York: Vintage Books, 1980) on the bourgeoisie and sexuality: 'This class must be seen ... as being occupied, from the mid-eighteenth century on, with creating its own sexuality and forming a specific body based on it, a 'class' body with its health, hygiene, descent, and race: the autosexualization of its body, the incarnation of sex in its body, the endogamy of sex and the body' (p. 124).

80. C.B. Wadström and August Nordenskiöld, *Plan for a free Community upon the Coast of Africa* (London, 1789), pp. 35-36 (Wadström and Nordenskiöld's italics).

81. Lynn Hunt, op. cit., pp. 35-37.

82. *Politics for the People*, Vol. 1, Part II, op. cit., p. 9, p. 10.

83. Ibid., p. 7.

84. Ibid., p. 7.

85. *The Life, Death, and Wonderful Atchievements of Edmund Burke. A New Ballad. By the Author of the Wrongs of Africa* (London, 1792), p. 4.

86. W.J.T. Mitchell, *Blake's Composite Art. A Study of the Illuminated Poetry* (Princeton, New Jersey: Princeton University Press, First Princeton paperback printing, 1982), p. 10.

87. Ibid., pp. 9-10.

88. Lynn Hunt, op. cit., p. 37.

89. *Aristotle The Poetics 'Longinus' On the Sublime Demetrius On Style*, The Loeb Classical Library No. 199 (London and Cambridge, Massachusetts: Heinemann and Harvard University Press, reprinted 1965), p. 125. Cf. also ibid., p. 165: 'Demosthenes' strength ... may ... be compared to a flash of lightning or a thunderbolt'.

90. Lynn Hunt, op. cit., p. 37.

91. Cf. ibid., p. 37.

92. *Liberty and Property Preserved Against Republicans and Levellers*, Number II (1792), p. 4.

93. *Réimpression de L'Ancien Moniteur*. Tôme vingt et unième (Paris, 1846), p. 355: '... cet homme si petit, qui voulait être si grand, et qui, s'il eût pu, aurait déplacé l'Eternel pour se mettre à sa place'.

94. Cf. also Gnostic myth concerning this quest for priority. In 'The Origin of the World' 'the ruler Yaldabaoth' (the demiurge) makes similar claims, but 'the authorities' laugh at his *hubris*: 'They laughed at the First Father because he lied, saying: "I am God. No one else exists before me"' (*The Nag Hammadi Library in English*, San Francisco, etc.: Harper & Row, 1981, p. 170).

95. Carol Blum, *Rousseau and the Republic of Virtue. The Language of Politics in the French Revolution* (Ithaca and London: Cornell University Press, Cornell Paperbacks, 1989), p. 252.

96. Ibid., p. 253.

97. Other Jacobins than Robespierre were also provided with the same kind of 'christomimetic' role. According to Louis R. Gottschalk, 'A well-defined *culte de Marat* sprang up' after the assassination of the latter, and 'Hymns were sung and speeches pronounced comparing him to Jesus - at least once to Jesus' disparagement' (*Jean Paul Marat. A Study in Radicalism*, Chicago and London: The University of Chicago Press, 1967, p. 187).

98. Friedrich Schlegel, '"Athenäums"-Fragmente', in: *Kritische und theoretische Schriften* (Reclam, 1978), p. 135. Cf. also Schlegel on Robespierre and his 'deification': 'Mirabeau hat eine grosse Rolle in der Revolution gespielt, weil sein Charakter und sein Geist revolutionär war; Robespierre, weil er der Revolution unbedingt gehorchte, ... *und sich für den Gott derselben hielt* ...' (ibid., p. 135, my italics).

99. Ronald Paulson, op. cit., p. 237.

100. Northrop Frye, op. cit., p. 223.

A Tinge of Superstition:
Tracing Wordsworth's Political and Philosophical Revolutions through French Radicalism to English Pastoralism and Conservatism, 1790-1818

Per Serritslev Petersen

[Oswald's] thirst after the extraordinary buoys him up, and, supported by a habit of constant reflexion, he frequently breaks out into what has the appearance of greatness; and, in sudden emergencies, when he is called upon by surprize & thrown out of the path of his regular habits, or when dormant associations are awakened tracing the revolutions through which his character has passed, in painting his former self he really *is* great. ... Having shaken off the obligations of religion & morality in a dark and tempestuous age, it is probable that such a character will be infected with a tinge of superstition.

William Wordsworth, 'Preface to *The Borderers*'[1]

Since the days of the French Revolution, one half of Europe has been referred to as the left, the other half as the right. Yet to define one or the other by means of the theoretical principles it professes is all but impossible. And no wonder: political movements rest not so much on rational attitudes as on the fantasies, images, words, and archetypes that come together to make up this or that *political kitsch*.

Milan Kundera, *The Unbearable Lightness of Being* (1984)[2]

As T. S. Eliot observed in *Four Quartets*, human kind cannot bear too much reality, and call it kitsch, superstition, life-lie or whatever, the fact remains that man has always seemed to need, as Saul Bellow's dangling man Joseph confesses to his alter ego *Tu As Raison Aussi*, an ideal construction, an obsessive device, 'some exclusive focus, passionate and engulfing', because that is 'the only possible way to meet chaos',[3] confront the ultimate nothingness of the human condition - the infinite void of the universe, as a Sartrean existentialist might have put it. At this point in the argument Saul Bellow (or Joseph) raises the interesting issue of 'the gap between the ideal construction and the real world, the truth'.[4] An interesting philosophical problem, to be sure, but only if you happen to be a so-called naive or common-sense realist, 'prostrate and overborne - as if the mind / Itself were nothing, a mean pensioner / On outward forms', to quote one of Wordsworth's many epistemological dicta in *The Prelude*.[5] If, on the other hand, you happen to be a romantic egotist[6] like the author-hero of the autobiographical *Prelude*, Wordsworth's idealized reconstruction of 'the discipline / And consummation of the poet's mind' (*Pre5* viii.270-71), you would hardly find the problem interesting or relevant at all. Indeed, knowledge, objective knowledge of the real world, 'present, actual, superficial life' (*Pre5* viii.652), came to be seen by Wordsworth as a highly problematic thing (the jealous God of the *Genesis* was of the same opinion, as it happens: thou shalt not eat of the tree of knowledge or...). For knowledge could be 'purchased with the loss of power' (*Pre5* v.449), 'a treasonable growth / Of indecisive judgements that impaired / And shook the mind's simplicity' (*Pre5* iii.214-16). So it was not knowledge as such that Wordsworth principally sought: he 'craved for power' (*Pre5* v.755), the existential clout of an ideal construction, passionate and engulfing, 'a Faith / That fails not, in all sorrow my support, / The blessing of my life' (*Pre99* ii.489-91). In this existential will-to-power game, the creative imagination, of course, is Wordsworth's prime agent: it is the ideal constructor, as it were, the glorious faculty that can 'build up greatest things / From least suggestions' (*Pre5* xiii.98-99). Imagination is 'but another name for absolute strength' (*Pre5* xiii.168), for being an agent of the one great mind (like Coleridge's 'primary imagination'), it 'creates, creator and receiver both' (*Pre99* ii.303), which means that it is 'by sensible impressions not enthralled, / But quickened, rouzed, and made thereby more fit / To hold communion with the invisible world' (*Pre5* xiii.103-5). And it is by virtue of its power to commune with the invisible world beyond present, actual, superficial life, that the creative imagination becomes the utopian imagination *par excellence*:

> ... In such strength
> Of usurpation, in such visitings
> Of awful promise, when the light of sense
> Goes out in flashes that have shown to us
> The invisible world, doth greatness make abode,
> There harbours whether we be young or old.

> Our destiny, our nature, and our home,
> Is with infinitude - and only there;
> With hope it is, hope that can never die,
> Effort, and expectation, and desire,
> And something evermore about to be.

(Pre5 vi.532-42)

But here again the interesting question of the gap between the ideal/utopian construction and the real world, between abstract and concrete potentiality,[7] crops up, if not for Wordsworth himself, then at least for the student of Wordsworth's political and philosophical career. Following the above celebration of the utopian imagination, Wordsworth makes a point of telling the reader that the mind beneath the militant banners of that imagination does not think of 'spoils or trophies, nor aught / That may attest its prowess' because it is

> ... blest in thoughts
> That are their own perfection and reward -
> Strong in itself, and in the access of joy
> Which hides it like the overflowing Nile.

(Pre5 vi.544-48)

However, this ivory-tower version of the utopian imagination, with its escapist note of quietism and solipsism, is flatly contradicted and refuted by the following statement of 'anti-utopian' enthusiasm and activism in Book X of *The Prelude*, where Wordsworth recollects the bliss of being alive, young and 'strong in love', in the brave new world of revolutionary France, 1790-92:

> ... they too, who, of gentle mood,
> Had watched all gentle motions, and to these
> Had fitted their own thoughts (schemers more mild,
> And in the region of their peaceful selves),
> Did now find helpers to their hearts' desire
> And stuff at hand plastic as they could wish,
> Were called upon to exercise their skill
> Not in Utopia - subterraneous fields,
> Or some secreted island, heaven knows where -
> But in the very world which is the world
> Of all of us, the place in which, in the end,
> We find our happiness, or not at all.

(Pre5 x.716-28)

How do we account for this contradiction, this tension between the quietism and solipsism of the utopian imagination hidden by an overflowing

78

Nile in some subterraneous 'Utopia' and the enthusiasm and activism of the utopian imagination belonging to this very world? Is it a case of philosophical ambivalence or confusion in the author-hero of *The Prelude*, or does Wordsworth actually mean to present us with, as an organic part of his autobiographical project, a plurality of conflicting characters and self-images? I think the answer is both-and, pell-mell. As a piece of mythopoeic self-idealization and self-glorification, a tour de force in what Keats called the Wordsworthean or egotistical sublime, *The Prelude* is not, after all, primarily concerned with autobiographical truth, and objective knowledge, as we have seen, was never a philosophical desideratum anyway. Wordsworth himself makes no bones about admitting that he cannot say 'what portion [of *The Prelude*] is in truth / The naked recollection of that time, / And what may rather have been called to life / By after-meditation' (*Pre5* iii.645-48). The psychological exposition of Oswald (quoted at the beginning of the essay), the revolutionary intellectual and villain in Wordsworth's blank-verse drama *The Borderers* (written 1796-97), is in many ways applicable to the author's own psychopathology. 'When dormant associations are awakened tracing the revolutions through which his character has passed, in painting his former self', Wordsworth, like Oswald, 'really *is* great'. Besides, sharing with Oswald the same existential trauma of 'a dark and tempestuous age', the author of *The Prelude* can be seen to be equally 'infected with a tinge of superstition'.[8] Thus the subject matter of *The Prelude* is unequivocally claimed to be 'in truth heroic argument' (*Pre5* iii.182), the epic hero being the poet himself as the chosen son of nature with 'holy powers and faculties' (*Pre5* iii.84-85), a 'dedicated spirit' (*Pre5* iv.344):

> ... Of genius, power,
> Creation and divinity itself,
> I have been speaking, for my theme has been
> What passed within me.
>
> (*Pre5* iii.171-74)

Now in tracing Wordsworth's political and philosophical revolutions from 1790 when revolutionary France was still 'standing on the top of golden hours, / And human nature seeming born again' (*Pre5* vi.352-55), the biographer will of course be obliged to use *The Prelude* (and other autobiographical poems like, for instance, *Descriptive Sketches* and 'Tintern Abbey') as a major source of biographical information. So faced with the problematic truth-value and epistemology of Wordsworth's 'biographic verse' (*Pre5* xiii.341), the biographer will also be saddled with the question of the gap between the ideal poetic construction and the truth, in other words, the hermeneutical problem of sifting the real Wordsworth, alive in the very world - which may be defined here as an historically authenticated world (however imperfect and tentative the authentication) - from Wordsworth's own mythopoeic recollections in tranquillity, his various post-festum reconstructions, revisions and elisions.

Revolution I: French Dances of Liberty and Youth, 1790-92

When Wordsworth, at the age of 20, clandestinely left England, for the first time in his life, to tour France, Switzerland, Italy and Germany (1,500 miles, mostly on foot), it was seen both by himself and his family as an act of rebellion. What did he rebel against in the summer of 1790? According to *The Prelude*, the scheme was 'an open slight / Of college cares and study' (the college being St John's College at Cambridge), though not 'entertained without concern for those / To whom my worldly interests were dear' (*Pre5* vi.342-345), 'without uneasy forethought of the pain, / The censures, and ill-omening' (*Pre50* vi.330-31) of his family. Wordsworth's mother and father had both died by the time he was 13, and, with his brothers and sister, he had since been dependent on his uncles, Richard Wordsworth of Whitehaven and Christopher Crackanthorpe Cookson, who as guardians administered all of the money for their daily living. The problematic nature of that dependence was no doubt exacerbated by Wordsworth's knowledge that had Sir James Lowther (Lord Lonsdale from 1784) paid the four and a half thousand pounds owing to his father when he died in his service, his lot would have been less humiliating. As his sister Dorothy, in a letter to her friend Jane Pollard, summed up the 'early misfortune' of the Wordsworth children: 'We in the same moment lost a father, a mother, a home, we have been equally deprived of our patrimony by the cruel Hand of lordly Tyranny'.[9] Wordsworth's poor academic performance at Cambridge, climaxing in the provocation of ignoring his family's advice 'to stick close to College for the first two or three years'[10] and instead spending 14 weeks of the long vacation touring Europe, must be viewed in the light of these traumatizing experiences. At Cambridge he felt 'detached / Internally from academic cares, / From every hope of prowess and reward' (*Pre5* vi.29-31). He decided not to read for Honours (thus in effect rejecting the fellowship that his family had intended for him),[11] and although this decision is romantically attributed to 'that over-love / Of freedom planted in me from the very first, / And indolence, by force of which I turned / From regulations' (*Pre5* vi.44-46), it seems evident that Wordsworth's lack of scholastic commitment must be seen as another act of rebellion against the guardians, who, by sending him to Cambridge, had settled him in a career of *their* choice: he was meant, in due course, to take holy orders, 'vegetating on a paltry curacy',[12] and he resented that. Going abroad, then, was the angry young man's rebellion against, and escape from, the oppressiveness of present, actual, superficial life - *his* human condition, the thought of which could sometimes make him tremble with 'an indefinite terror and dismay' (*Pre5* viii.660).

'Bliss was it in that dawn to be alive, / But to be young was very heaven!' (*Pre5* x.692-93). Actually, it was not so much the attraction of revolutionary France as 'a country in romance' (*Pre5* x.696) that made him go abroad that summer in 1790, it was youth, 'the ever-living universe / And independent spirit of pure youth' (*Pre5* vi.701-2) -

... Nature then was sovereign in my heart,
And mighty forms seizing a youthful fancy
Had given a charter to irregular hopes.
In any age, without an impulse sent
From work of nations and their goings-on,
I should have been possessed by like desire;

(*Pre5* vi.346-51)

Wordsworth and his undergraduate friend Robert Jones happened to cross from Dover to Calais on July 13, so they arrived in France 'on the very eve / Of that great federal day' (*Pre5* vi.356-57), that is, July 14, on which the anniversary of the fall of the Bastille was celebrated, and Louis XVI pledged allegiance to the new democratic constitution at an altar erected in the Champ de Mars. However, Wordsworth was not particularly interested in the French Revolution and its festivities at this stage of his political and philosophical career: as a Continental tourist he was bound for the Alps, the Alpine sublimities of English eighteenth-century pastoralism, while revolutionary France, with its 'benevolence and blessedness / Spread like a fragrance everywhere' (*Pre5* vi.368-69), its 'dances of liberty' (*Pre5* vi.381) beneath the evening star, was merely a picturesque sideshow:

During the time which was near a month which we were in France [Wordsworth wrote his sister Dorothy from Switzerland], we had not once to complain of the smallest deficiency in civility in any person, much less of any positive rudeness. We had also perpetual occasion to observe that chearfulness and sprightliness for which the French have always been remarkable. But I must remind you that we crossed it at the time when the whole nation was mad with joy, in consequence of the revolution. It was a most interesting period to be in France, and we had many delightful scenes where the interest of the picture was owing solely to this cause.[13]

The real goal of Wordsworth's Continental tour was the 'sublime and beautiful objects'[14] of Alpine nature, which are duly catalogued in the same long letter to Dorothy. Here he declares himself 'a perfect Enthusiast'[15] in his admiration of nature in all her various forms, especially 'the more awful scenes of the Alps',[16] which, predictably, turn his soul from the thought of man and any single created being to 'him who produced the terrible majesty'[17] of the landscape.

At a later date, Wordsworth's grand tour would be recollected in tranquillity and become idealized/poeticized into *Descriptive Sketches* (1793), complete with Rousseauesque pastoralism and republicanism. But before that could happen, he had to complete his studies at Cambridge (an undistinguished BA in January 1791) and return to France once more. After spending most of the year in London, convinced that he was 'doomed to be an idler thro[ughou]t his life',[18] he somehow managed to be advised by his guardians 'to pass the Time previous to the Time of his Taking Orders in some retired Place in France',[19] and on 26 November 1791 he crossed the Channel to Dieppe. His destination was Orléans, 'led thither', according to the more flattering biographical account in *The Prelude*, 'chiefly by a personal wish / To speak the language more familiarly' (*Pre5* ix.36-37). On the way he visited revolutionary Paris and saw its various spots of 'recent fame' (*Pre5* ix.42), the Champ de Mars, the Panthéon, the Bastille, the 'clamorous halls' (*Pre5* ix.46) of the National Assembly and the Jacobin Club, but he did so 'in the guise / Of an enthusiast ... affecting more emotion' (*Pre5* ix.66-67, 71) than he really felt. Like other intellectuals, he claims to have read the English 'master pamphlets of the day' (*Pre5* ix.97), that is, the major texts in the so-called revolution debate or controversy[20] - Edmund Burke's *Reflections on the Revolution in France* (1790), Mary Wollstonecraft's *Vindication of the Rights of Men* (1790), Thomas Paine's *Rights of Man*, Part I (1791), and James Mackintosh's *Vindiciae Gallicae* (1791). But still he felt 'unprepared / With needful knowledge' (*Pre5* ix.92-93) when he first encountered the ongoing political and philosophical debates in Orléans: 'all things were to me / Loose and disjointed, and the affections left / Without a vital interest' (*Pre5* ix.106-8). While in Orléans, Wordsworth seems to have been exposed to the whole gamut of opinions in revolutionary France, from the conservatism of the royalist *emigrés* to the uncompromising radicalism of the jacobins. As an Englishman and 'stranger, with youth's further privilege' (*Pre5* ix.194), he could live and talk freely with the defenders of the crown, who tried their best to bring him over to their cause. But it was all to no avail, for 'though untaught by thinking or by books / To reason well of polity or law' (*Pre5* ix.201-2), Wordsworth had the good fortune of being born in the poor Lake District, which 'retaineth more of ancient homeliness, / Manners erect, and frank simplicity, / Than any other nook of English land' (*Pre5* ix.219-20). With his birthright of 'sub-servience from the first / To God and Nature's single sovereignty' (*Pre5* ix.238-39) and 'mountain liberty' (*Pre5* ix.242), supplemented with his recent experience of Cambridge as 'a republic, where all stood thus far / Upon equal ground, that they were brothers all' (*Pre5* ix.230-1), Wordsworth was bound to be impervious to the rhetoric of 'the regal sceptre, and the pomp / Of orders and degrees' (*Pre5* ix.212-13). A natural democrat from the Lake District, Wordsworth had always hailed as best 'the government of equal rights / And individual worth' (*Pre5* ix.248-49), so why should he make a great fuss of the French Revolution?

> If at the first great outbreak I rejoiced
> Less than might befit my youth, the cause
> In part lay here, that unto me the events
> Seemed nothing out of nature's certain course -
> A gift that rather was come late than soon.
> No wonder then if advocates like these
> Whom I have mentioned, at this riper day
> Were impotent to make my hopes put on
> The shape of theirs, my understanding bend
> In honour to their honour. Zeal which yet
> Had slumbered, now in opposition burst
> Forth like a Polar summer ...
>
> (*Pre5* ix.250-61)

Things were no longer loose and disjointed, his affections no longer without a vital interest. The royalists of Orléans had helped to awaken his slumbering zeal, and he had at long last found his ideal construction in these matters, his exclusive focus, passionate and engulfing. Wordsworth became a patriot, a jacobin, enthusiastically committed to the French Revolution: 'my heart was all / Given to the people, and my love was theirs' (*Pre5* ix.124-25). But he had also found himself a devoted friend and mentor in his political-philosophical awakening and conversion, viz. the 37-year-old, nobly born Michel Beaupuy, captain in the 32nd (Bassigny) regiment, 'with an oriental loathing spurned' (*Pre5* ix.297) by the other officers in the regiment for being a patriot. Beaupuy was not a mere college friend, with whom he could have philosophical discussions about 'rational liberty and hope in man, / Justice and peace' (*Pre5* ix.402-3), he belonged to the real world of action beyond the academic groves of 'thoughts abstruse' (*Pre5* ix.404) -

If Nature then be standing on the brink
Of some great trial, and we hear the voice
Of one devoted, one whom circumstance
Hath called upon to embody his deep sense
In action, give it outwardly a shape,
And that of benediction to the world.
Then doubt is not, and truth is more than truth -
A hope it is and a desire, a creed
Of zeal by an authority divine
Sanctioned, of danger, difficulty, or death.

$\qquad\qquad\qquad\qquad\qquad\qquad\qquad\qquad$ (*Pre5* ix.405-414)

A creed of zeal, danger and death: in the dark and tempestuous age of the
French Revolution, Wordsworth, like Oswald in *The Borderers*, had evidently been infected with a tinge of superstition, a touch of religious obsession,
complete with a martyrdom complex. Willingly would he 'have taken up /
A service at this time for cause so great, / However dangerous' (*Pre5* x.134-
36), and if he had not returned to England (in late November or early
December 1792), 'compelled by nothing less than absolute want / Of funds
for my support' (*Pre5* x.190-1), he 'doubtless should have made a common
cause / With some who perished, haply perished too' (*Pre5* x.194-95).

In view of the fact that the psychodynamics of religious conversion -
in the *Moniteur* obituary, his mentor Beaupuy was actually recalled as the
personification of 'l'esprit religieux de la Revolution'[21] - and the
psychodynamics of falling in love are so similar, it is hardly a coincidence
that Wordsworth's account of his political and philosophical 'consciousness-
raising' in Book IX of the 1805 *Prelude* is concluded with the tragic love
story of *Vaudracour and Julia* (later published as a separate poem and
excluded from *The Prelude*). There appears to be a consensus of critical
opinion about the autobiographical significance of this peculiar narrative
within the context of the 1805 *Prelude*: '*Vaudracour and Julia* stands in
lieu of an account of his relationship with Annette Vallon, whom he met ca.
January 1792, and by whom he had a child, christened in Orleans Cathedral
on December 15 as Anne-Caroline Wordsworth'.[22] But what makes
Vaudracour and Julia so unique is the fact that it is the only place in his
work where, as Émile Legouis was the first to point out, Wordsworth
describes *con amore* 'the intoxication of passion',[23] celebrates the 'balmy
time' (*Pre5* ix.557) of youthful love, the 'fascination' (*Pre5* ix.582) of being
in love. After his 'delirious hour' (*Pre5* ix.597) as Vaudracour in 1792,
Wordsworth, at least as a poet, 'turned to a formal puritan, / A solemn and
unsexual man', to quote Shelley's satirical portrait in *Peter Bell the Third*
(1819).[24] But, as Émile Legouis also points out, in omitting Annette Vallon

from *The Prelude*, Wordsworth 'at the same time did away with all that made the pathetic complexity of those summer months'[25] - *and* spring months as well, in so far as Anne-Caroline must have been conceived around her father's birthday, April 7. The 'pathetic complexity' of Wordsworth's French radicalism could, I think, be cited as a perfect illustration of the thesis propounded by Henry, Tom Stoppard's cynical protagonist in *The Real Thing* (1982), viz. that 'public postures have the configuration of private derangement',[26] and it is only by combining the psychopathologies of religious conversion and erotic passion, thus appreciating Wordsworth's poetic condensation of carnal and political-philosophical knowledge, that the reader can start making sense of the sound and fury of, for instance, the following passage in *The Prelude*:

> O pleasant exercise of hope and joy,
> For great were the auxiliars which then stood
> Upon our side, we who were strong in love.
> Bliss was it in that dawn to be alive,
> But to be young was very heaven! O times,
> In which the meagre, stale, forbidding ways
> Of custom, law, and statute took at once
> The attraction of a country in romance -
>
> (*Pre5* x.689-96)

In his semi-authorized *Memoirs of William Wordsworth* (1851), Christopher Wordsworth, the bishop and the poet's nephew, discreetly covered up the love affair and its consequences. He could not, however, resist moralizing, in more general terms, on his uncle's critical condition in revolutionary France, and then the cat is almost let out of the bag: 'an orphan, young, inexperienced, impetuous, enthusiastic', Wordsworth had found himself in a foreign country where 'the most licentious theories were propounded; all restraints were broken; libertinism was the law'.[27] But the cover-up had of course started long before when Wordsworth himself anticipated his nephew the bishop's Victorian puritanism, not only by suppressing an account of the relationship in Book IX of *The Prelude*, but, even earlier perhaps, through his 'reactionary' characterization of the revolutionary Oswald as 'having shaken off the obligations of religion and morality in a dark and tempestuous age'.[28]

Revolution II: One of That Odious Class of Men Called Democrats, 1792-95

Soon after Wordsworth returned to England, Louis XVI was guillotined in Paris (21 January 1793), and about a week later *An Evening Walk* and *Descriptive Sketches* were published in London. Wordsworth had 'huddled up those two little works and sent them into the world' because, as he later explained to his friend William Mathews: 'as I had done nothing by which to distinguish myself at the university, I thought these little things might shew that I could do something'.[29] As noted above, *Descriptive Sketches* represents a pastoral idealization of Wordsworth's Continental walking tour in 1790, embedded as the poem is in a traditional eighteenth-century pastoralism, a rhetoric and ideology which, in John Williams's words, sought 'an analogue for social order in the natural world, revealing by degrees the mind of an omnipotent creator whose ultimate purposes remained shrouded in mystery'.[30] Closely allied to this pastoral rhetoric and ideology, we find the following expression of Rousseauesque primitivism-cum-republicanism (Wordsworth is here eulogizing the Swiss peasant and his 'independent happiness'):[31]

> Once, Man entirely free, alone and wild,
> Was blest as free - for he was Nature's child.
> He, all superior but his God disdained,
> Walked none restraining, and by none restrained:
> Confessed no law but what his reason taught,
> Did all he wished, and wished but what he ought.
> As man in his primeval dower arrayed
> The image of his glorious Sire displayed,
> Even so, by faithful Nature guarded, here
> The traces of primeval Man appear;[32]

At the end of the poem Wordsworth's pastoral politics is updated into a more specific sense of political programme, viz. a millenarian commitment to the cause of the French Revolution, in which he also seems to endorse revolutionary violence (the September Massacres, if not the execution of Louis XVI) as a means to an end, the end being the glorious liberation and regeneration of Europe:

> Rejoice, brave Land, though pride's perverted ire
> Rouse hell's own aid, and wrap thy fields in fire:
> Lo, from the flames a great and glorious birth;
> As if a new-made heaven were hailing a new earth.[33]

However, in Wordsworth's open letter to Richard Watson, Bishop of Llandaff, the composition of which must have been started immediately after the publication of *Descriptive Sketches* (but never completed or published), no holds are barred in his militant championship of the French Revolution. In *Appendix to A Sermon Preached before the Stewards of the Westminster Dispensary* (dated 25 January 1793), Watson, who had earlier welcomed the French Revolution in two pamphlets of 1790 and 1791, expressed his horror at Louis XVI's execution and cautiously aligned himself with Burke in his defence of the British constitution:

> That the constitution of this country is so perfect as neither to require or admit of any improvement, is a proposition to which I never did or ever can assent; but I think it far too excellent to be amended by peasants and mechanics.[34]

In his polemical *Letter to the Bishop of Llandaff* Wordsworth first deplores the fact that Watson, the liberal 'bishop of the dissenters' (*Prose I* 31), should 'attach so much importance to the personal sufferings of the late royal martyr' that he could not refrain from 'joining the idle cry of modish lamentation which has resounded from the court to the cottage' (*Prose I* 32). Besides, the passion of pity is 'one of which, above all others, a christian teacher should be cautious of cherishing the abuse' (*Prose I* 32). The passion of pity should always, Wordsworth argues within the traditional debate on the operation of the passions in human nature, be under the influence of reason and be 'regulated by the disproportion of the pain suffered to the guilt incurred' (*Prose I* 33). Rational people should only feel sorry for the fallen monarch because the prejudice and weakness of mankind have made it necessary to force an individual into an unnatural situation, which requires more than human talents and human virtues: 'any other sorrow for the death of Louis is irrational and weak' (*Prose I* 33). Wordsworth then goes on to tax Watson with his ignorance of the nature of man because he should have known that 'a time of revolution is not the season of true Liberty':

> Alas! the obstinacy & perversion of men is such that she [i.e., liberty] is too often obliged to borrow the very arms of despotism to overthrow him [i.e. despotism], and in order to reign in peace must establish herself by violence. (*Prose I* 33)

Watson had once approved of the objective which 'the French had in view when in the infancy of the revolution they were attempting to destroy arbitrary power and to erect a temple to liberty on its ruins' (*Prose I* 35), so how could he now presume to dictate to the world a servile adoption of the British constitution? Watson is, Wordsworth concludes, 'guilty of a most glaring contradiction' (*Prose I* 35). In his Burkean aversion to republicanism

Watson had asserted that a republic is the most oppressive to the bulk of the people because they are deceived with a show of liberty, but they actually live 'under the most odious of all tyrannies, the tyranny of their equals' (*Prose* 35). This argument makes Watson an ally of the 'infatuated moralist' Mr Burke, the author of the counter-revolutionary *Reflections on the Revolution in France*, who, 'in a philosophic lamentation over the extinction of Chivalry, told us that in those times vice lost half its evil, by losing all its grossness' (*Prose* 35-36).[35] But slavery is slavery, Wordsworth rejoins, and it is a bitter and poisonous draught: 'we have but one consolation under it - that a nation may dash the cup to the ground when she pleases' (*Prose* 36). However, because taught from infancy that they are born in a state of inferiority to their oppressors, the bulk of mankind is 'even more ready to lay themselves under the feet of *the great*, than the great are to trample upon them' (*Prose* 36). Reflecting on the degraded state of the mass of mankind, a philosopher can only lament that oppression is not odious to them, as Rousseau had done in a famous passage in *The Social Contract* (1762), and Wordsworth then clinches the argument by quoting, in French, his French philosopher of radicalism:

Tout homme né dans l'esclavage nait pour l'esclavage: rien n'est plus certain: les esclaves perdent tout dans leurs fers, jusqu'au désir d'en sortir; ils aiment leur servitude, comme les compagnons d'Ulysse aimaient leur abrutissement.

(*Prose* 36)

Wordsworth also addresses Watson's aristocratic scepticism about peasants' and mechanics' political qualifications and points out that the administration of a republican form of government would require 'much less of what is usually called talents and experience, that is of disciplined treachery and hoary machiavelism' (*Prose* 39). The virtues, intellectual and otherwise, of Swiss and French peasantry are then adduced in a passage that rhetorically merges Wordsworth's pastoral and revolutionary politics:

If your lordship has travelled in the democratic cantons of Switzerland you must have seen the herdsman with the staff in one hand and the book in the other. In the constituent assembly of France was found a peasant whose sagacity was as distinguished as his integrity, whose blunt honesty overawed and baffled the refinements of hypocritical patriots.

(*Prose* 39)

Watson, who had, in Wordsworth's words, expressed 'enthusiastic fondness of the judicial proceedings' (*Prose* 47) of his country, is ironically congratulated on his having so far passed through life without having his fleece torn from his back in the thorny labyrinth of litigation. It is undoubtedly Wordsworth's early experience of litigation from the cruel hand of lordly tyranny (as Dorothy so nicely put it) that prompts his scathing observations on nobility and its titles, stars, ribbands, garters and 'other badges of fictitious superiority' (*Prose1* 44). Such arbitrary distinctions and separations among mankind are 'absurd, impolitic, and immoral' (*Prose1* 44) because they entail 'the necesssity of dissimulation which we have established by regulations which oblige us to address as our superiors, indeed as our masters, men whom we cannot but internally despise' (*Prose1* 45). Finally, Watson is again coupled with Burke in his eulogy of the British constitution. Where Mr Burke had roused the indignation among all enlightened men, 'when by a refinement in cruelty superiour to that which in the East yokes the living to the dead he strove to persuade us that we and our posterity to the end of time were riveted to a constitution by the indissoluble compact of a dead parchment' (*Prose1* 48), Watson is now aiming at the same detestable object by 'attempting to lull the people of England into a belief that any enquiries directed towards the nature of liberty and equality can in no other way lead to their happiness than by convincing them that they have already arrived at perfection in the science of government' (*Prose1* 48). Wordsworth and his friends of liberty will generously abstain from insinuating that Watson has 'partaken of Mr Burke's intoxicating bowl'. They will content themselves, shaking their heads as he staggers along, with remarking that he has 'business on both sides of the road' (*Prose1* 49).

The London Wordsworth had returned to after his year in France was the London of British jacobinism, and by far the most important of the many radical societies and clubs that had been founded in 'the climate of political excitement created in Britain by the dramatic and astonishing events in France'[36] was the London Corresponding Society (LCS). *A Letter to the Bishop of Llandaff* proves beyond any doubt that Wordsworth, after his one-year education in French jacobinism, had become an enthusiastic British jacobin, insisting on the inalienable natural rights of all men (the rights to life, property and the pursuit of happiness), emphasizing the equal political rights of all men, and condemning hereditary honours, titles and privileges. Later in the year he started composing his anti-war poem 'Salisbury Plain' (revised and published in 1842 under the title of 'Guilt and Sorrow'), and here the revolutionary enlightenment project of jacobinism is spelt out in the concluding exhortation of the early version:

Heroes of Truth pursue your march, uptear
Th'Oppressor's dungeon from its deepest base;
High o'er the towers of Pride undaunted rear
Resistless in your might the herculean mace

Of Reason; let foul Error's monster race
Dragged from their dens start at the light with pain
And die; pursue your toils, till not a trace
Be left on earth of Superstition's reign...[37]

However, the poem remained unpublished, as did *A Letter to the Bishop of Llandaff*, and so contributed nothing to the cause of British jacobinism. Unlike Coleridge and Southey, the radical Wordsworth, as Stephen Gill notes in his biography, 'never acquired a public identity'.[38]

France had declared war on England and Holland on 1 February 1793, and during the following spring and summer, according to *The Prelude*, 'the strength of Britain was put forth / In league with the confederated host' (*Pre5* x.229-30), the confederated host being the coalition of England and various continental powers, notably Prussia and Austria. The Wordsworth of *The Prelude* received, on that occasion, an unprecedented shock to his moral nature, a lapse or turn of sentiment that 'might be named / A revolution' (*Pre5* x.236-37). Up till now he had played with the breeze, 'a green leaf on the blessed tree / Of my beloved country' (*Pre5* x.254-55), but the war with 'regenerated France' (*Pre5* x.244) cut him off from that pleasant station, and he rejoiced, exulted 'when Englishmen by thousands were o'erthrown, / Left without glory on the field' (*Pre5* x.261-62). It must, indeed, have been a 'truth painful to record' (*Pre5* x.259) for the post-revolutionary poet, but the truth was that, in that tempestuous age of his life, Wordsworth was, as he proudly told his friend William Mathews in the spring of 1794, 'of that odious class of men called democrats',[39] and of that class, he swore, he would for ever continue. His political credo was prompted by Mathews's suggestion that they and another young man should found 'a monthly miscellany from which some emolument might be drawn',[40] and Wordsworth thought they ought not to be ignorant of each others' political sentiments. His next letter to Matthews on the same issue reads like a political and philosophical manifesto as if he was already composing an editorial for their journal:

> I disapprove of monarchical and aristocratical governments, however modified. Hereditary distinctions and privileged orders of every species I think must necessarily counteract the progress of human improvement: hence it follows that I am not amongst the admirers of the British constitution.[41]

Wordsworth, however, has become much more wary of revolution and revolutionary violence than he was in *Descriptive Sketches* and *A Letter to the Bishop of Llandaff*. The subversion of the British constitution is almost a foregone conclusion, but now the actual destruction of those institutions that he is condemning appears to him 'to be hastening on too rapidly', and he 'recoil[s] from the bare idea of a revolution'.[42] And when Wordsworth goes on to argue that it is a duty incumbent upon every enlightened friend of mankind to 'slip no opportunity of explaining and enforcing those general principles of the social order which are applicable to all times and places', and to 'diffuse by every method a knowledge of [the] rules of political justice',[43] it becomes fairly obvious that William Godwin must have replaced Michel Beaupuy as Wordsworth's political and philosophical guru. No other work in his time, William Hazlitt claimed, had given 'such a blow to the philosophical mind of the country as the celebrated *Enquiry Concerning Political Justice*',[44] and Godwin, who, as a utopian rationalist, believed that 'it is to the improvement of reason [...] that we are to look for the improvement of our social condition',[45] had also made a point of warning against the tyranny of revolution with its 'peculiar aggravations':[46]

... revolutions, instead of being truly beneficial to man kind, answer no other purpose, than that of marring the salutary and uninterrrupted progress, which might be expected to attend upon political truth and social improvement. They disturb the harmony of intellectual nature. They propose to give us something, for which we are not prepared, and which we cannot effectually use. They suspend the wholesome advancement of science, and confound the process of nature and reason.[47]

Corresponding to Godwin's basic propositions that 'soundness of understanding is connected with freedom of enquiry',[48] and that 'sound reasoning and truth, when adequately communicated, must always be victorious over error',[49] we may cite the following statement in Wordsworth's letter:

Freedom of enquiry is all that I wish for; let nothing be deemed too sacred for investigation; rather than restrain the liberty of the press I would suffer the most atrocious doctrines to be recommended: let the field be open and unencumbered, and truth must be victorious.[50]

In the end the scheme for the journal dedicated to Godwinian freedom of enquiry came to nothing. Apart from money, one good reason for the abortion of the scheme could have been the one suggested by Wordsworth's brother Richard in a letter: 'I hope you will be cautious in writing or expressing your political opinions. By the suspension of the Habeas Corpus Acts the Ministers have great powers'.[51] The Habeas Corpus was suspended in May 1794, and the Act was part of the Government's repressive legislation and adminstration, Pitt's 'reign of terror', which 'thirsted to make the guardian crook of law / A tool of murder' (*Pre5* x.646-47) in order to destroy the leadership of the radical societies, silence the radical propagandists, and frighten the rank and file into abandoning the reform movement.[52]

In 1794 Wordsworth, however, was reasonably far from the madding crowd of radical London. William Calvert, a boyhood friend from the Lake District, had generously offered him and his sister Dorothy his farmhouse Windy Brow on the slopes above Keswick, and although he wanted to be nearer the political and philosophical centre of the country, he could not afford to move to London without a job. Later in the year 'a sense of duty'[53] detained him in the Lake District when another friend and generous benefactor in the Calvert family, Raisley Calvert, the younger brother of William Calvert, became seriously ill with tuberculosis. Evidently Wordsworth was not ready yet to embark on Revolution III, his pastoral return-to-nature project, and he longed to be back in the metropolis of English civilization:

> I begin to wish much [he wrote his London friend William Mathews in the autumn of 1794] to be in town; cataracts and mountains, are good occasional society, but they will not do for constant companions; besides I have not even much of their conversation, and still less of that of my books as I am so much with my sick friend, and he cannot bear the fatigue of being read to.[54]

About a month after Raisley Calvert's funeral on 12 January 1795 Wordsworth was back in London, where he appears to have associated with most of the famous radicals of the day, including the author of the *Enquiry Concerning Political Justice* and that rationalistic 'philosophy / That promised to abstract the hopes of man / Out of his feelings, to be fixed thenceforth / For ever in a purer element' (*Pre5*. x.806-9).

Revolution III: Pastoral Coverts Interposed Betwixt the Heart of Man and the Uneasy World, 1795-1813

As Christopher Gill points out in his biography, place names are used in an interesting way in most accounts of Wordsworth's poetic development. When identifying moments of artistic growth in, say, Dickens or Yeats, critics usually refer to particular books, but lovers of Wordsworth are 'at least as likely to mark out the poet's spiritual odyssey by referring to 'Windy Brow', 'Racedown', 'Alfoxden', 'Dove Cottage', 'Rydal Mount''.[55] I propose to follow this convention, and the pastoral coverts of the title may be identified as Racedown (where Wordsworth lived from September 1795), Alfoxden and Dove Cottage (from which he moved in May 1813).

Godwin did not last long as Wordsworth's political and philosophical sage. In a letter to William Mathews from March 1796, Wordsworth humorously discusses the possibility of Dorothy and himself being transformed into cabbages at Racedown, which is bound to happen eventually, if rural retirement in its full perfection, complete with planting cabbages, 'be as powerful as one of Ovid's Gods'.[56] He concludes the letter by commenting on the second edition of Godwin's *Enquiry Concerning Political Justice* (1796), which he had expected to find much improved. But he has not been encouraged in this hope by the perusal of the second preface, which is all he has looked into so far:

> Such a piece of barbarous writing I have not often seen. It contains scarce one sentence decently written. I am surprized to find such gross faults in a writer who has had so much practise in composition.[57]

What had happened since the days of the grand scheme for a Godwinian journal? And where did Wordsworth find his political and philosophical alternative to Godwinian rationalism? Judging from *The Prelude*, Wordsworth appears to have lost his philosophical nerve when he actually tried to implement his Godwinian enlightenment project. He had ambitiously pursued a higher nature -

> ... wished that man should start
> Out of the worm-like state in which he is,
> And spread abroad the wings of Liberty,
> Lord of himself, in undisturbed delight.
>
> (*Pre5* x.835-39)

But he got perplexed, 'sacrificed / The exactness of a comprehensive mind / To scrupulous and microscopic views' (*Pre5* x.843-45), and turned into a mad scientist:

> ... I took the knife in hand,
> And, stopping not at parts less sensitive,
> Endeavoured with my best of skill to probe
> The living body of society
> Even to the heart. I pushed without remorse
> My speculations forward, yea, set foot
> On Nature's holiest places.
>
> (*Pre5* x.872-78)

Political science as a sacrilegious vivisection of nature, setting foot where angels fear to tread. No wonder Wordsworth got 'endlessly perplexed / With impulse, motive, right and wrong, the ground of moral obligation' (*Pre5* x.894-96) and eventually lost

> All feeling of conviction, and, in fine,
> Sick, wearied out with contrarieties,
> Yielded up moral questions in despair,
> And for [his] future studies, as the sole
> Employment of the inquiring faculty,
> Turned towards mathematics, and their clear
> And solid evidence.
>
> (Pre5 x.898-904)

Wordsworth did not become a mathematician after all. But it is worth remembering perhaps that, according to Book VI of *The Prelude*, mathematical studies had always fascinated and comforted him in his youth because 'transcendent peace did await upon these thoughts' (*Pre5* vi.157-58), and because the simple, pure proportions and relations of geometric science presented him with 'an image not unworthy of the one / Surpassing life, which - out of space and time, / Nor touched by welterings of passion - is, / And hath the name of, God' (*Pre5* vi.154-57). But after the spiritual desiccation of Godwinian rationalism-cum-atheism Wordsworth needed a more substantial religion to sink his teeth into, not a mathematical or philosophical God. For he was never cut out to be a philosopher in the classical sense of, say, Leo Strauss, who distinguished between 'the sweet solace of religion' and the 'savage truth' of philosophy (while Christ weeps, Socrates the philosopher laughs). It was Samuel Taylor Coleridge that presented him with the religious and metaphysical construction, passionate and engulfing, that he needed at this critical moment of his life, 'didst lend a living help / To regulate [his] soul' (*Pre5* x.906-7). Like Oswald in *The Borderers*, Wordsworth's Godwinian self had only recognized 'the immediate law / From the clear light of circumstances flashed / Upon an independent Intellect',[58] but the price he had had to pay for that independent intellect was what Coleridge, in his poem 'Religious Musings' (1794), had diagnosed as a godless 'Anarchy of Spirits' devoid of 'the moral world's cohesion'.[59] Godwinian man *was*, Wordsworth must have felt in the dark night of his soul, Coleridge's godless man, 'disherited of soul' and with 'no common centre':

> ... A sordid solitary thing,
> Mid countless brethren with a lonely heart
> Through courts and cities the smooth savage roams
> Feeling himself, his own low self the whole;
> When he by sacred sympathy might make

The whole one Self! Self, that no alien knows!
Self, far diffused as Fancy's wing can travel![60]

And considering the pastoral pantheism celebrated in 'Tintern Abbey', Wordsworth's 'sense sublime / Of something far more deeply interfused', one can imagine how he must have thrilled at the image of the One Life in Coleridge's 'The Eolian Harp' (1796):

And what if all of animated nature
Be but organic Harps diversely fram'd,
That tremble into thought, as o'er them sweeps
Plastic and vast, one intellectual breeze,
At once the Soul of each, and God of all?[61]

It is all there in the early poems of Coleridge, what could be termed the ideological and psychological matrices of Wordsworth as pantheistic 'worshiper of Nature', including his slumbers of cosmic ecstasy and identity: 'all self-annihilated', the 'drowséd Soul' of 'Religious Musings' will 'make / God its Identity: God all in all'.[62] Even the 'ethics' of the pantheistic *unio mystica*, which is assumed to account for the 'best portion of a good man's life' (to stick to 'Tintern Abbey' as one of the manifestos of Revolution III), Wordsworth could have appropriated from 'Religious Musings':

... 'Tis the sublime of man,
Our noontide Majesty, to know ourselves
Parts and proportions of one wondrous whole!
This fraternises man, this constitutes
Our charities and bearings.[63]

What Wordsworth chose not to appropriate, however, was Coleridge's vested interest in Christian dogma. Although an active political radical, 'a Democrat & a Seditionist',[64] Coleridge always insisted on being 'a zealous Partisan of Christianity, a Despiser & Abhorrer of French Philosophy & French Morals',[65] while his dear friend Wordsworth was, alas, 'a Republican & at least a *Semi*-atheist'.[66] In 1794 the radical Wordsworth had considered priesthood the profession attended with the greatest inconveniences,[67] and his anticlericalism seems to have survived at least the first years of Revolution III, in so far as the topic of Christian dogma is taboo in Wordsworth's and Coleridge's discussions at Racedown or Alfoxden - at least that is how I interpret Coleridge's words: 'on one subject we are habitually silent'. Coleridge is writing to the Reverend John Prior Estlin, who is reassuringly informed that Wordsworth after all still 'loves &

venerates Christ & Christianity'. But then Coleridge significantly adds: 'I wish, he did more'.[68]

Otherwise Wordsworth's pastoral retirement, his withdrawal into the West Country, Racedown in Dorset and Alfoxden in Somerset, must be seen as an urgently needed escape from the increasingly uncongenial world of political radicalism and philosophical rationalism, the 'over-pressure of the times / And their disastrous issues' (*Pre5* xi.47-48), which had brought him to the verge of a nervous breakdown. Nature's self, assisted by human love, viz. that of Dorothy and Coleridge, had now returned him to his 'earlier life', given him back 'strength and knowledge full of peace, / Enlarged, and never more to be disturbed' (*Pre5* x.924-26). Book XI of 1805 *Prelude* opens with a hymn to his pastoral paradise regained, the 'breezes and soft airs that breathe / The breath of paradise' (*Pre5* xi.10-11), the brooks and the

```
        ... groves, whose ministry it is
To interpose the covert of [their] shades,
Even as a sleep, betwixt the heart of man
And the uneasy world - 'twixt man himself,
Not seldom, and his own unquiet heart -
```

(Pre5 xi.15-19)

Again Coleridge, as his new philosophical mentor (later to be acknowledged by Wordsworth as one of the two persons to whom his intellect was most indebted),[69] may have provided the blueprint for this pastoralism-cum-escapism philosophy. Like Wordsworth, Coleridge had been a committed young radical, but, unlike Wordsworth, he had acquired a public identity as political lecturer and editor. He had eventually retired from radical politics and politicking to settle in the West Country (at the end of 1796): 'I have [he confessed to his brother, Reverend George Coleridge] snapped my squeaking baby-trumpet of Sedition & the fragments lie scattered in the lumber-room of Penitence'.[70] Instead he had withdrawn himself almost totally from the consideration of immediate causes to muse on the *causae causarum*, devoting himself to 'such works as encroach not on the anti-social passions'.[71] But already in an interesting letter from March 1795, Coleridge is actively considering and philosophizing about the pastoral way of life as an alternative to his city life:

It is melancholy to think, that the best of us are liable to be shaped & coloured by surrounding Objects - and a demonstrative proof, that Man was not made to live in Great Cities! Almost all the physical Evil in the World depends on the existence of moral Evil - and the long-continued contemplation of the latter does not tend

96

to meliorate the human heart. - The pleasures, which we receive from rural beauties, are of little Consequence compared with the Moral Effect of these pleasures - beholding constantly the Best possible we at last become ourselves the best possible. In the country, all around us smile Good and Beauty - and the Images of this divine χαλοχἀγαθόν are miniatured on the mind of the beholder, as a Landscape on a Convex Mirror. [James] Thompson in that most lovely Poem, the Castle of Indolence, says -

> ['']I care not, Fortune! what you me deny -
> You cannot rob me of free Nature's Grace!
> You cannot shut the Windows of the Sky,
> Through which the Morning shews her dewy face -
> You cannot bar my constant feet to rove
> Through Wood and Vale by living Stream at Eve'[72]

The letter is interesting, I think, not only because it documents Coleridge's philosophical and psychological preoccupation with pastoralism at this early stage, but also because it points to James Thomson's Augustan pastoralism by way of illustration. It was Thomson who, in his preface to *Winter* (1726), one of his four poems on the seasons, had confessed that he knew of 'no subject more elevating, more amusing, more ready to awake the poetical enthusiasm, the philosophical reflection, and the moral sentiment, than the works of Nature', and he came to epitomize the eighteenth-century pastoral tradition in which also Wordsworth was born and bred as a poet: not only the author of the juvenilia, *An Evening Walk*, *Descriptive Sketches* and 'Salisbury Plain', but also, after Dorothy had 'preserved [him] still / A poet' (*Pre5* x.918-19), the author of *Lyrical Ballads* (1798). Indeed, we should dismiss at the outset, as Marilyn Butler suggests in *Romantics, Rebels and Reactionaries*, 'the belief, still widely held, that Wordsworth's contributions to the *Lyrical Ballads* of 1798 represent an altogether new kind of poetry'.[73] His famous preface to *Lyrical Ballads*, with its humanistic (and moralistic) emphasis on the essential simplicity and 'worthy *purpose*' of poetry, is basically true to the spirit of neoclassicism and actually represents 'a remarkably complete statement of what the artist's Neoclassical revolution might mean for the poet dedicated and consistent enough to carry it through in terms of his principal tool, language'.[74] In terms of political and existential philosophy, however, Wordsworth's 'neoclassical revolution' as a pastoral poet also entailed reaction and regression into quietism, escapism and primitivism. John Williams admirably sums up the ideological implications of neoclassical pastoralism proper:

> The landscape poet was committed to a piously foregone conclusion about the evidence of God's handiwork in nature throughout its infinitely variable forms; this assumption was in turn readily transferred to reflections on the nature of social

and political order. Human society, with its vast differences of degree and privilege, was understood to have a place within the whole order of creation, and to offer the student of mankind an edifying microcosm of that creation.[75]

In what some hostile reviewers considered Wordsworth's less edifying romantic version of pastoralism,[76] pantheism may be said to have replaced deism, but in both cases God and nature are treated almost synonymously. It is within the microcosm of romantic pastoralism (as distinct from radicalism) that we must place what Nicholas Roe has called the 'paradigm for Wordsworth's larger development from poet of protest to poet of human suffering'.[77] But Wordsworth's post-revolutionary paradigm comprises not only Roe's poet of human suffering. There is also the poet of pastoral equipoise or self-protective composure, the poet that, in Book I of *The Excursion* (1814), celebrates the splendid rural isolation of the Wanderer, 'a lone Enthusiast':

> Itinerant in this labour, he had passed
> The better portion of his time; and there
> Spontaneously had his affections thriven
> Amid the bounties of the year, the peace
> And liberty of nature; there he kept
> In solitude and solitary thought
> His mind in a just equipoise of love.
> Serene it was, unclouded by the cares
> Of ordinary life; unvexed, unwarped
> By partial bondage. In his steady course,
> No piteous revolutions had he felt,
> No wild varieties of joy and grief.[78]

Equipoise of *love*? A contradiction in terms? Whatever, Wordsworth's ideal construction of romantic pastoralism[79] spells escapism, primitivism, quietism. The ultimate quietus is the unconscious condition of sleep (hinted at in the image of the pastoral covert interposed 'even as a sleep') and death: 'I long for a repose that ever is the same' ('Ode to Duty'), the sublime epitaph of Lucy beyond 'the touch of earthly years' ('A Slumber Did My Spirit Seal') - the pastoral death-wish of English romanticism that later was to culminate in Tennyson's 'Give us long rest or death, dark death, or dreamful ease' ('The Lotos-Eaters'). After Revolution III, Wordsworth can no longer be called a poet in the Keatsian sense of the word, that is, one of 'those to whom the miseries of the world / Are misery, and will not let them rest': as a Keatsian dreamer, Wordsworth has found himself a pastoral haven in a world of 'mock lyrists, large self-worshipers'.[80]

If Wordsworth was no longer a poet of radical protest, he could still be engaged in politics, not party politics, though, at this stage, but pastoral politics, that is, as a philosopher-poet commenting, from his rural retreats in the West Country and (from December 1799) the Lake District, on the condition of England and the world. His disillusionment with English as well as French radicalism, the betrayal of the French Revolution climaxing in the summons of a pope 'to crown an Emperor - / This last opprobrium, when we see the dog / Returning to its vomit' (*Pre5* x. 933-35), triggered off a series of patriotic sonnets, dedicated to 'national independence and liberty',[81] and celebrating England and Englishness, past and present, while, at the same time, denigrating France and Frenchness, past and present:

> Great men have been among us; hands that penned
> And tongues that uttered wisdom - better none:
> The later Sidney, Marvel, Harrington,
> Young Vane, and others who called Milton friend.
> These moralists could act and comprehend:
> They knew how genuine glory was put on;
> Taught us how rightfullly a nation shone
> In splendour: what strength was, that would not bend
> But in magnanimous meekness. France, 'tis strange
> Hath brought forth no such souls as we had then.
> Perpetual emptiness! unceasing change!
> No single volume paramount, no code,
> No master spirit, no determined road;
> But equally a want of books and men![82]

Also Wordsworth the chauvinistic sonneteer, enthusing about the perfect bliss of treading again the grass of his native English soil ('Composed in the Valley near Dover'), had his fair share of superstition - curiously enough, it was in Goslar, Germany, in the last quarter of 1798, that he first articulated his post-Godwinian, almost Lawrentian *Blut-und-Boden* anti-intellectualism: 'I know no book or system of moral philosophy written with sufficient power to melt into our affection[? s], to incorporate itself with the blood & vital juices of our minds'.[83] In 1808-9, however, political sonneteering was superseded by pamphleteering when Wordsworth became so obsessed with the so-called Convention of Cintra that he wrote a whole book, complete with scholarly appendix, about 'the political injustice and moral depravity which are stamped upon the front of this agreement' (*Prose1* 264).[84] The agreement or convention had been negotiated between a British and a French army to conclude a minor Napoleonic war in Portugal, but what made the affair so traumatizing to English patriots back home was the fact that, although it was the British army, commanded by Wellesley, that had defeated the French, the routed French troops had nevertheless been allowed, by the terms of Articles II and V of the Convention, to 'evacuate Portugal with their arms and baggage', not to be 'considered as prisoners of war', and to carry with them 'equipments, and all that is comprehended under the name of property of the army' (*Prose* 352). The political and philosophical argument of Wordsworth's pamphlet *The Convention of Cintra*, subtitled 'The whole brought to the test of those Principles, by which alone the Independence and Freedom of Nations can be Preserved or Recovered' (*Prose* 220), is a curious hodgepodge of millenarian enthusiasm (harking back to Beaupuy's *esprit religieux*), post-Godwinian anti-intellectualism, *Blut-und-Boden* primitivism and nationalism (dating from his recent phase of patriotic sonneteering), and the occasional note of philosophical realism.

It is Wordsworth the pastoral philosopher-poet who, 'in the solitude of a peaceful vale', has written down the truths that he has been meditating as 'a private individual' (*Prose* 336). Like Petrarch, whose *De Vita Solitaria* he quotes at the end of the pamphlet, Wordsworth self-consciously creates the pastoral persona of himself as

> ... a man of disciplined spirit, who withdrew from the too busy world - not out indifference to its welfare, or to forget its concerns - but retired for wider compass of eyesight, that he might comprehend and see in just proportions and relations; knowing above all that he, who hath not first made himself master of the horizon of his own mind, must look beyond it only to be deceived.
>
> (*Prose* 342)

The pastoral and millenarian perspectives of the argument are elegantly fused in Wordsworth's quotation from Virgil's famous return-of-the-golden-age eclogue (IV): 'Magnus ab integro seclorum nascitur ordo' etc. (*Prose* 297).[85] Also the noble peasant of romantic pastoralism - 'the very peasant in the field', to whose eyes the sublime truths of human nature are invariably laid open (*Prose* 298) - is duly summoned to denounce the infamous Convention of Cintra, and what it stands for, viz. 'an utter want of *intellectual* courage' in the British generals (*Prose* 256), who had been motivated by prosaic considerations like 'the great importance of gaining time; fear of an open beach and equinoctial gales for shipping; fear that reinforcements could not be landed; fear of famine; - fear of everything but dishonour!' (*Prose* 254). The French *should* have been subdued on this truly providential occasion, their ferocious warfare and heinous policy confounded, not, Wordsworth insists *sub specie aeternitatis pastorali*, to liberate the soil, the cities and forts of Portugal, but 'for the rights of human nature which might be there conspicuously asserted' (*Prose* 261). True to his romantic epistemology of the creative imagination and its ideal/utopian constructions, Wordsworth is not particularly concerned with the present, actual, superficial life of the real world, real countries and cities like Portugal and Lisbon. A Derridean deconstructionist *manqué* ('Il n'y a pas de hors texte'!), he is principally concerned with *language*, the poetic language of symbolic gestures in the dreamland of pastoral politics:

> We [i.e., the British troops in Portugal] combated for victory in the empire of reason, for strong-holds in the imagination. Lisbon and Portugal, as city and soil, were chiefly prized by us as a *language*, but our Generals mistook the counters of the game for the stake played for.
>
> *(Prose1* 261-62)

But then generals will be generals, and the Convention of Cintra only shows 'how much the intellectual and moral constitution of our military officers, has suffered by a profession, which, if not counteracted by admonitions willingly listened to, and by habits of meditation, does, more than any other, denaturalize - and therefore degrade the human being' *(Prose1* 264). Not only the minds of generals, but also those of statesmen, particularly such as are high in office, are *a priori* 'unfavourable to the growth of this knowledge' *(Prose1* 304), that is, a thorough knowledge of human nature. If governors better understood 'the rudiments of nature as studied in the walks of common life', they could also better 'calculate upon the force of the grander passions' *(Prose1* 306-7). For let the fire of those grander passions break out afresh, let but the human creature, 'whether he have lain heedless and torpid in religious or civil slavery - have languished under a thraldom, domestic or foreign', be roused, let him rise and act, and his imagination and affections will 'from that moment participate the dignity of the newly ennobled being whom they will now acknowledge for their master' *(Prose1* 294). The grand passions, 'these mighty engines of Nature' *(Prose1* 292), are the *religious* passions of the people - Wordsworth instances 'the marvellous atchievements which were performed by the first enthusiastic followers of Mohammed' *(Prose1* 294). Again it is the noble peasant, with his strong *Blut-und-Boden* roots, that personifies the ideal of a religious and patriotic people:

> [The peasant's] intellectual notices are generally confined within narrower bounds: in him no partial or antipatriotic interests counteract the force of those nobler sympathies and antipathies which he has in right of his Country; and lastly the belt or girdle of his mind has never been stretched to utter relaxation by false philosophy, under a conceit of making it sit more easily and gracefully.
>
> *(Prose1* 328)

The bottom line of this argument appears to be that it is quite safe for the British to support Spain and Portugal in their heroic struggle against French tyranny because the Spanish and Portuguese peoples are *safe*: they are noble peasants, temperamentally disposed for patriotism, not French radicalism, 'Jacobinism' (*Prose* 332). Industrialization and urbanization has not yet 'denaturalized' or corrupted the Spanish people, 'inflamed their passions by intemperance' (*Prose* 332). Madrid is not an enormous city like Paris, overgrown and disproportionate, 'sickening and bowing down, by its corrupt humours, the frame of the body politic' (*Prose* 332):

> Nor has the pestilential philosophism of France made any progress in Spain. No flight of infidel harpies has alighted upon their ground. A Spanish understanding is a hold too strong to give way to the meagre tactics of the 'Système de Nature;' or to the pellets of logic which Condillac has cast in the foundry of national vanity, and tosses about at hap-hazard - self-persuaded that he is proceeding according to art. The Spaniards are a people with imagination: and the paradoxical reveries of Rousseau, and the flippancies of Voltaire, are plants which will not naturalise in the country of Calderon and Cervantes.
>
> (*Prose* 332)

They are, of course, a superstitious people, these Catholic peasants, but although Spanish bigotry leaves much to be lamented, Wordsworth is confident that he has already 'proved that the religious habits of the nation must, in a contest of this kind, be of inestimable service' (*Prose* 332).

The occasional note of philosophical or psychological realism is struck when Wordsworth acknowledges that the grand passions and magnificent desires of the religious zealot can be 'attractive for their own sakes' and dispose the mind 'to regard commotion with complacency, to watch the aggravations of distress with welcoming' (*Prose* 307). We may even register a note of sobering self-examination when Wordsworth has to confess that it is not 'desirable as an absolute good, that men of comprehensive sensibility and tutored genius - either for the interests of mankind or for their own - should, in ordinary times, have vested in them political power' (*Prose* 307).

Revolution IV and Conclusion: a Sedate Yielding to the Pressure of Existing Things, 1813-18

One of the more important things Wordsworth had to yield to before he (to deploy again the symbolism of Wordsworthean place-names) could move from Dove Cottage to Rydal Mount in May 1813, was the generous patronage of the new Lord Lonsdale, the heir and cousin of the old Lord

Lonsdale, who, with his cruel hand of lordly tyranny, had once deprived the Wordsworth family of their patrimony. In a letter to Lord Lonsdale, Wordsworth explains, in some detail, how he has been disappointed in his hope that the profits of his literary labours added to the little he possessed would have answered to the rational wants of himself and his family. He had erroneously calculated upon the degree in which his writings were likely to suit the taste of the times. However, the objective of 'the statement of these facts' was, as his Lordship would probably have anticipated

> ... that if any Office should be at your Lordship's disposal (the duties of which would not call so largely upon my exertions as to prevent me from giving a considerable amount of time to study) it might be in your Lordship's power to place me in a situation where with better hope of success I might advance towards the main object of my life; I mean the completion of my literary undertakings...[86]

In April 1813 Wordsworth became, thanks to the power of his Lordship, Distributor of Stamps for Westmorland and the Penrith area of Cumberland and thus an agent of the administrative state apparatus. Historically and ideologically speaking, Wordsworth has come full circle with Revolution IV, in so far as he has now returned to the fold of (neo)classical pastoralism and paternalism, where once his father and grandfather had conscientiously, as Wordsworth reminds his Lordship in the letter, 'discharge[d] such trusts as were reposed in them through that [feudal] connection'.[87] In the coming years Wordsworth would serve his noble lord equally conscientiously, not only as a Distributor of Stamps, and not 'just for a handful of silver' (as Robert Browning would have it),[88] but because he really had passed through that last political and philosophical revolution and become a truly Burkean *laudator temporis acti*, paying homage - as he does, for instance, in his electioneering pamphlet *Two Addresses to the Freeholders of Westmorland* (1818) - to the British constitution as 'a mellowed feudality' (*ProseIII* 175), and pleading for 'an humble reliance on the wisdom of our Forefathers, and a sedate yielding to the pressure of existing things' (*ProseIII* 181). Burke, incidentally, did not make the two early versions of *The Prelude*, but, in Book VII of the 1850 *Prelude*, the genius of Burke is rehabilitated by 'the pen seduced / By specious wonders' (*Pre50* vii.512-13) - Wordsworth had not forgotten his earlier defamation of Mr Burke in *A Letter to the Bishop of Llandaff*. The reactionary author of *Reflections on the Revolution in France* is now praised for his eloquent denunciation of 'all systems built on abstract rights' (*Pre50* vii.524), for his celebration of 'the vital power of social ties / Endeared by Custom' (*Pre50* vii.527-28), and for his 'exploding upstart Theory' (*Pre50* vii.529).

That Wordsworth really meant business as the new Tory vassal of Lord Lonsdale, his involvement with the Westmorland election of 1818 demonstrates with a vengeance. The Lonsdales had always nominated the two county candidates (on this occasion Lord Lonsdale's own two sons, Viscount Lowther and Colonel Henry Lowther), but this time Henry Brougham, a radical Whig 'from the dirty alleys and obscure courts of the Metropolis' (*Prose III* 171), had come to contest pastoral Westmorland in the general election. As a Tory freeholder in his own right, and as Lord Lonsdale's loyal vassal, Wordsworth took the matter very seriously indeed. He canvassed for the Lonsdale candidates, wrote various letters to the local press, and published the *Two Addresses to the Freeholders of Westmorland*. According to the second of these addresses, Mr Brougham, the smart lawyer-politician from London, was not only a radical Whig of the old Foxite brand, 'captivated by the vanities of a system founded upon abstract rights' (*Prose III* 157) and sharing 'the alarming attachment of that Party [i.e, the Whigs] to French theories' (*Prose III* 162), he was an ultra-radical Whig to boot, 'labouring to ingraft certain sour cuttings from the wild wood of ultra reform, on the reverend, though somewhat decayed stock of [the] tree of Whiggism' (*Prose III* 163). And the 'presumptuous spirit' of ultra-radicalism, French or English, is given very short shrift after Wordsworth's Revolution IV:

> The independence which they [i.e., ultra-radical demagogues like Mr Brougham] boast of despises habit, and time-honoured forms of subordination; it consists in breaking old ties upon new temptations; in casting off the modest garb of private obligation to strut in the glittering armour of public virtue; in sacrificing, with jacobinical infatuation, the near to the remote, and preferring to what has been known and tried, that which has no distinct existence, even in imagination; in renouncing, with voluble tongue and vain heart, every thing intricate in motive, and mixed in quality, in a downright passion of love for absolute, unapproachable patriotism!
>
> (*Prose III* 170)

Freeholders have always known that their rights were most likely to repose in safety 'under the shade of rank and property' (*Prose III* 176), where 'authority like the parental, from a sense of community of interest and the natural goodness of mankind, is softened into brotherly concern' (*Prose III* 186). But the new candidate, Mr Brougham, has reportedly mentioned, at a dinner given, at the London Tavern, to the Friends of Parliamentary Reform, 'the two radical doctrines of *yearly election*, and the *Franchise enjoyed by all paying taxes*' (*Prose III* 178). Although Mr Brougham has, on other occasions, denounced 'the *combined* doctrines of Annual Parliaments and Universal Suffrage, as chimerical and absurd'

(*ProseIII* 179), he has, Wordsworth insinuates in his pamphleteering polemics, been very close to recommending both at the London Tavern (another symbolically significant place-name, to be sure!), and 'such a union is equally suitable to an age of gross barbarism, and an age of false philosophy' (*ProseIII* 179). So, politically as well as philosophically, Wordsworth's apostasy was complete by 1818, despite his own indignant claim, three years later, that whereas others had been deluded by places and persons, he had 'stuck to Principles'.[89] In E. P. Thompson's words, Wordsworth had fallen back 'within the forms of paternalistic sensibility', 'within the traditional frame of paternalism, Anglican doctrine, fear of change'.[90]

By way of conclusion, I should perhaps point out that my attempt to analyse Wordsworth's political and philosophical development from 1790 to 1818 in terms of four revolutions (no more, no less!) must be seen as an essentially heuristic device, seeing that the demarcation lines between the various phases of his development are invariably blurred by, for instance, the restraints and demands imposed by the specific genre or discourse that Wordsworth happened to choose as his medium (poetry, essays, pamphlets etc.). Besides, 'who shall', as Wordsworth asked himself in *The Prelude*, 'parcel out / His intellect by geometric rules' (*Pre5* ii.208-9)? That said, let me try and summarize the overall argument by concluding that after his acute disillusionment with Godwinian rationalism as an ideal construction, which could somehow make sense of his ambivalent experiences of French and English politics, Wordsworth lost his philosophical nerve: he could not bear the lightness of enlightened being *à la* Kundera because he simply was not cut out for the heroics of philosophical rationalism. Nor did he consider it a duty, as Godwin had argued in *Enquiry Concerning Political Justice*, 'to make proper advantage of circumstances as they arise, and not withdraw [himself], because everything is not conducted according to [his] ideas of propriety'.[91] Infected with a tinge of romantic superstition, he opted for the epistemological irrationalism of the Coleridgean imagination and the quietism or conservatism of pastoral poetics and politics.

Notes

1. Owen, W.J.B., and Smyser, J.W. (eds), *The Prose Works of William Wordsworth*, 3 vols, Oxford 1974, Vol. I, p. 78. Hereafter cited in the text and the notes as *ProseI*, *ProseII* and *ProseIII* respectively. Wordsworth wrote the preface to *The Borderers* between 1796 and 1800.
2. Kundera, Milan, *The Unbearable Lightness of Being*, London 1985, p. 257.

3. Bellow, Saul, *Dangling Man*, Harmondsworth 1971, p. 116.
4. Ibid.
5. Wordsworth, J., Abrams, M.H., and Gill, S. (eds), *William Wordsworth: The Prelude 1799, 1805, 1850*, New York 1979, p. 224 (*Prelude* 1805 vi.666-67). Hereafter cited in the text as *Pre99*, *Pre5* and *Pre50* respectively.
6. According to George Santayana, the programme of the 'romantic egotist' is to absorb the whole world. Absolute egotism in Goethe and Emerson 'summoned all nature to minister to the self: all nature, if not actually compelled to this service by a human creative fiat, could at least be won over to it by the engaging heroism of her favourite child' ('Hints of Egotism in Goethe', in Henfrey, N. (ed), *Selected Critical Writings of George Santayana*, 2 vols, Cambridge 1968, Vol. I, p. 184).
7. Cf. Georg Lukács on the distinction between concrete and abstract potentialities in 'The Ideology of Modernism': 'Abstract potentiality belongs wholly to the realm of subjectivity; whereas concrete potentiality is concerned with the dialectic bewteen the individual's subjectivity and objective reality' (*The Meaning of Contemporary Realism*, London 1969, pp. 23-24).
8. See note 1.
9. Dorothy Wordsworth to Jane Pollard, 16 February 1793. In Selincourt, E.D. (ed.), *Letters of William and Dorothy Wordsworth; The Early Years, 1787-1805*, rev. Shaver, C.L., Oxford 1967, p. 88. Hereafter cited as *EY*.
10. John Robinson to William Wordsworth, 6 April 1788. *EY* 18 (note 4).
11. *William Wordsworth: The Prelude 1799, 1805, 1850*, p. 188 (note 6).
12. William Wordsworth to William Mathews, 23 September 1791. *EY* 59.
13. William Wordsworth to Dorothy Wordsworth, 6 and 16 September 1790. *EY* 36.
14. *EY* 32.
15. *EY* 35.
16. *EY* 34.
17. *EY* 34.
18. William Wordsworth to William Mathews, 23 November 1791. *EY* 62.
19. Richard Wordsworth (brother) to Richard Wordsworth of Whitehaven (uncle), 7 November 1791. *EY* 61 (note 1).
20. See Marilyn Butler on 'the pamphlet war in the 1790's': 'As a public issue, the 'Revolution debate' lasted for about six years, from the first English rejoicings at France's new dawn in 1789, to December 1795, when Pitt's government introduced measures to stop the spread of radicalism by the printed and spoken word' (Butler, M. (ed.), *Burke, Paine, Godwin and the Revolution Controversy*, Cambridge 1984, p. 1).
21. *Moniteur* xxix.168. Quoted in Roe, N., *Wordsworth and Coleridge: The Radical Years*, Oxford 1988, p. 55.
22. *William Wordsworth: The Prelude 1799, 1805, 1850*, p. 340 (note 2).
23. Legouis, É., *William Wordsworth and Annette Vallon*, London 1967 (first published 1922), p. 15.
24. Hutchinson, T. (ed.), *The Complete Poetical Works of Percy Bysshe Shelley*, Oxford 1960, p. 358.
25. *William Wordsworth and Annette Vallon*, p. 21.
26. Tom Stoppard, *The Real Thing*, London 1982, p. 34.
27. Quoted in Gill, S., *William Wordsworth: A Life*, Oxford 1989, p. 435 (note 107).
28. See note 1.

29. William Wordsworth to William Mathews, 23 May 1794. *EY* 120.
30. Williams, J., *Wordsworth: Romantic Poetry and Revolution Politics*, Manchester 1989, p. 4.
31. Hutchinson, T. (ed.), *The Poetical Works of Wordsworth*, rev. Selincourt, E.D., Oxford 1959, p. 14 (line 424).
32. Ibid. (lines 433-42).
33. Ibid., p. 17 (lines 642-45).
34. *Burke, Paine, Godwin, and the Revolution Controversy*, p. 147.
35. Edmund Burke's lamentation deserves to be quoted in full: 'But the age of chivalry is gone. - That of sophisters, oeconomists, and calculators, has succeeded; and the glory of Europe is extinguished for ever. Never, never more, shall we behold that generous loyalty to rank and sex, that proud submission, that dignified obedience, that subordination of the heart, which kept alive, even in servitude itself, the spirit of exalted freedom. The unbought grace of life, the cheap defence of nations, the nurse of manly sentiment and heroic enterprize is gone! It is gone, that sensibility of principle, that chastity of honour, which felt a stain like a wound, which inspired courage whilst it mitigated ferocity, which ennobled whatever it touched, and under which vice itself lost half its evil, by losing all its grossness' (Penguin Classics (1988), p. 170).
36. Dickinson, H.T., *British Radicalism and the French Revolution 1789-1815*, Oxford 1988, p. 6.
37. Quoted in *William Wordsworth: A Life*, p. 76.
38. Ibid., p. 73.
39. William Wordsworth to William Mathews, 23 May 1794. *EY* 119.
40. *EY* 118.
41. William Wordsworth to William Mathews, 8 June 1794. *EY* 123-124.
42. *EY* 124.
43. *EY* 124.
44. William Hazlitt, 'William Godwin', *The Spirit of the Age*, London 1825, p. 33.
45. Godwin, W., *Enquiry Concerning Political Justice*, ed. Carter, K.C., Oxford 1971, p. 15 ('Summary of Principles'). The first edition of the *Enquiry* was published in February 1793.
46. Ibid., p. 136 (Book IV, Chapter II: 'Of Revolutions').
47. Ibid., p. 138.
48. Ibid., p. 15 ('Summary of Principles').
49. Ibid., p. 55 (Book I, Chapter V: 'The Voluntary Actions of Men Originate in their Opinions').
50. *EY* 125.
51. Richard Wordsworth to William Wordsworth, 23 May 1794. *EY* 121 (note 4, *EY* 120).
52. See *British Radicalism and the French Revolution 1789-1815*, pp. 37-42.
53. William Wordsworth to William Mathews, 7 November 1794. *EY* 136.
54. *EY* 136.
55. *William Wordsworth: A Life*, p. 94.
56. William Wordsworth to William Mathews, 21 March 1796. *EY* 169.
57. *EY* 17.
58. *The Poetical Works of Wordsworth*, p. 50 (lines 1494-95).

59. Coleridge, E.H. (ed.), *The Poems of Samuel Taylor Coleridge*, Oxford 1960, p. 114 (lines 145-146).
60. Ibid. (lines 147-155).
61. Ibid., p. 102 (lines 44-48).
62. Ibid., pp. 110-111 (lines 34, 43-44).
63. Ibid., pp. 113-114 (lines 126-130).
64. Samuel Taylor Coleridge to George Coleridge, 10 March 1798. In Griggs, E.L., *Collected Letters of Samuel Taylor Coleridge*, 6 vols., Vol. I, Oxford 1956, p. 397.
65. Samuel Taylor Coleridge to Sir George and Lady Beaumont, 1 October 1803. In *Collected Letters of Samuel Taylor Coleridge*, Vol. II, Oxford 1956, p. 1002.
66. Samuel Taylor Coleridge to John Thelwall, 13 May 1796. In *Collected Letters of Samuel Taylor Coleridge*, Vol. I, p. 216.
67. William Wordsworth to William Mathews, 17 February 1794. *EY* 112.
68. Samuel Taylor Coleridge to John Prior Estlin, 18 May 1798. In *Collected Letters of Samuel Taylor Coleridge*, Vol. I, p. 410.
69. William Wordsworth to William Rowan Hamilton, 25 June 1832. In *Letters of William and Dorothy Wordsworth; The Later Years, 1829-1834*, rev. Hill, A.G., Oxford 1979, p. 536: 'He [i.e., Coleridge] and my beloved Sister are the two Beings to whom my intellect is most indebted'.
70. Samuel Taylor Coleridge to George Coleridge, 10 March 1798. In *Collected Letters of Samuel Taylor Coleridge*, Vol. I, p. 397.
71. Ibid.
72. Samuel Taylor Coleridge to George Dyer, 10 March 1795. In *Collected Letters of Samuel Taylor Coleridge*, Vol. I, p. 154-155.
73. Butler, M., *Romantics, Rebels and Reactionaries: English Literature and its Background 1760-1830*, Oxford 1981, p. 58.
74. Ibid., p. 59.
75. *Wordsworth: Romantic Poetry and Revolution Politics*, p. 3.
76. The less-edifying-Wordsworth or romantic-pastoralism-as-radicalism thesis was argued most forcefully by Francis Jeffrey, the notorious editor and reviewer of the *Edinburgh Review*.
77. *Wordsworth and Coleridge: The Radical Years*, p. 137.
78. *The Poetical Works of Wordsworth*, p. 595 (lines 345-360).
79. Wordsworth's romantic pastoralism *was* an ideal construction. What real country people were like at Racedown, as opposed to the pastoralized peasants, we may catch a glimpse of in a letter from 1795: 'We [i.e., Wordsworth and Dorothy] are both as happy as people can be who live in perfect solitude. We do not see a soul. Now and then we meet a miserable peasant in the road or an accidental traveller. The country people here are wretchedly poor; ignorant and overwhelmed with every vice that usually attends ignorance in that class, viz - lying and picking and stealing &c &c.' (William Wordsworth to William Mathews, 24 October 1795. *EY* 154).
80. John Keats, *The Fall of Hyperion*, Canto I, esp. lines 147-153, 197-200, 207. In Garrod, H.W. (ed.), *The Poetical Works of John Keats*, London 1960, pp. 406, 408.
81. *The Poetical Works of William Wordsworth*, p. 241.
82. Ibid., p. 244.
83. '[Essay on Morals]', *ProseI* 103.

84. Wordsworth's *Convention of Cintra* was published in May 1809, the complete title being *Concerning the Relations of Great Britain, Spain, and Portugal, to Each Other, and to the Common Enemy, at this Crisis; and Specifically as Affected by the Convention of Cintra* (*Prose1* 221).
85. In E. V. Rieu's translation of Virgil's eclogues, the millenarian lines quoted by Wordsworth run as follows: 'Time has conceived and the great Sequence of the Ages starts afresh. Justice, the Virgin, comes back to dwell with us, and the rule of Saturn is restored. The Firstborn of the New Age is already on his way from high heaven down to earth' (Virgil, *The Pastoral Poems*, Harmondsworth 1961, p. 55).
86. William Wordsworth to Lord Lonsdale, 6 February 1812. In *Letters of William and Dorothy Wordsworth; The Middle Years, 1812-1820*, rev. Moorman, M., and Hill, A.G., Oxford 1970, p. 3.
87. Ibid., p. 3.
88. See the opening lines of 'The Lost Leader', Browning's poem about Wordsworth the apostate: 'Just for a handful of silver he left us, / Just for a riband to stick in his coat'. In *The Poetical Works of Robert Browning*, London 1962, p. 208.
89. William Wordsworth to James Losh, 4 December 1821. In *The Letters of William and Dorothy Wordsworth; The Later Years, 1821-1828*, rev. Hill, A.G., Oxford 1978, p. 97.
90. Thompson, E.P., 'Disenchantment or Default? A Lay Sermon', *Power & Consciousness*, ed. O'Brien, C.C., and Vanech, W.D., London 1969, pp. 175, 176.
91. *Enquiry Concerning Political Justice*, p. 139 (Book IV, Chapter II: 'Of Revolutions').

Byron and the French Revolution

Jørgen Erik Nielsen

When the news of the fall of the Bastille on July 14, 1789 reached England, George Gordon Byron was 18 months old. When he became the sixth Lord Byron in 1798, the intervening years had seen the executions of Louis XVI and Marie Antoinette, Robespierre's reign of terror, and Napoleon Bonaparte's early victorious campaigns. The following year, in November 1799, Bonaparte assumed power in France and forced his adversaries assembled in the Second Coalition to conclude peace. In England the government had felt obliged to introduce various repressive measures against insurrection such as the suspension of the Habeas Corpus in 1794. The poet's mother had expressed sympathy with the popular cause in the French Revolution,[1] but when her son began taking an interest in politics the revolution proper and its repercussions were yesterday's events and republican France was moving towards rule by one man with expansionist inclinations.

However, Napoleon's assumption of power did not amount to the undoing of all the changes brought about in the years of revolution; neither did the restoration of the monarchy in 1815. Still, the latter event has to posterity come to mark the end of the years of turmoil, so the 'French Revolution' can be taken to embrace the years from 1789 to 1815. By using the term in this wider sense we get it to include years when Byron was an observer of current affairs, and we use it in the sense that appears to be

The Dolphin 19
©Aarhus University Press 1990

similar to his conception of it. In *Childe Harold's Pilgrimage*, IV, 97 he settled the accounts of developments in France in this way:[2]

> But France got drunk with blood to vomit crime,
> And fatal have her Saturnalia been
> To Freedom's cause, in every age and clime ...

Earlier in the same poem (III, 82) he had explained more fully what had gone wrong:

> But good with ill they also overthrew,
> Leaving but ruins, wherewith to rebuild
> Upon the same foundation, and renew
> Dungeons and thrones, which the same hour re-fill'd,
> As heretofore, because ambition was self-will'd.

According to the introductory letter to Canto IV, the narrator of the poem is 'the author speaking in his own person', so we have it on the best authority that these words express Byron's attitude around 1818. (In this case he appears to be serious, which is not always easy to determine). Altogether there are very few references to the decade following 1789 or to the leading figures of the Revolution in his diaries and letters, and the same is true about his poetry, but from his letter to Murray of February 16, 1821 we know that he then intended to have Don Juan decapitated in Paris during the Reign of Terror.

Napoleon, on the other hand, is often mentioned by Byron. What the great poet thought of the great general and later emperor has been of interest to many scholars and has even been made the subject of special studies.[3] Byron appears to have been an avid reader of newspapers, and in *Lord Byron und Napoleon* (p. 3) Gerhard Eggert assumes that he first became aware of Napoleon when the defeat of the Austrians by the French at Lodi in Lombardy on May 10, 1796 was reported in English newspapers. Napoleon displayed military genius as well as great personal courage in that battle. At any rate, that was the event that Byron reverted to when in his journal for April 9, 1814 he commented on the stunning news that the Emperor had abdicated: 'Yet to outlive *Lodi* for this!!!'[4] The next day he wrote 'Ode to Napoleon Buonaparte', which expresses his feelings on the abdication: he was disappointed that the great man should have agreed to spend the rest of his life 'in a very ambiguous state, between an Emperor and an Exile', as one of the mottoes of the ode has it (from Gibbon's narrative of the fate of the Emperor Nepos). Both in his prose writings and in the Ode Byron reproaches the French Emperor with having clung to 'the high command' too long, and both here and elsewhere it is evident that there was much hero-worship in Byron's high esteem of Napoleon. In his schooldays at Harrow he owned a bust of Bonaparte, which he had to defend against his school comrades, as he says in his journal for November 17, 1813; and on March 6, 1814 he informs us in his diary that he had sent his 'fine print of Napoleon to be framed' and afterwards admired the Emperor, who 'becomes his robes as if he had been hatched in them.' In the former entry Byron declares that ever since 1803 'he has been a *Héros de Roman* of mine - on the Continent; I don't want him here.' But his hero-worship had not prevented Byron from exulting on June 22, 1809 in a letter to his mother at the news of the Tyrolese revolt against Napoleon; and on his grand tour he had realized that to most Spanish people the Emperor was a foreign invader, which attitude finds expression in *Childe Harold's Pilgrimage*, I, e.g. 'Gaul's Vulture' (52). Byron's attitude to Napoleon appears to have been full of vacillation and contradiction, but in the instances here discussed he undoubtedly found it more important to side with peoples struggling against foreign dominance than to praise the great man, whom he admired at a safe distance, but did not want in England.

However, in 'Ode to Napoleon Buonaparte' there is more than worship of the great man, who proved a puny thing in the end, and recognition that he had also been a cruel warrior. Stanza 10 runs like this:

And Earth hath spilt her blood for him,
Who thus can hoard his own!
And Monarchs bow'd the trembling limb,
And thank'd him for a throne!
Fair Freedom! we may hold thee dear,
When thus thy mightiest foes their fear
In humblest guise have shown.
Oh! ne'er may tyrant leave behind
A brighter name to lure mankind!

Napoleon had exposed the abject frailty of European thrones; in that sense he had served the cause of freedom.

John Murray, Byron's publisher, solicited three additional stanzas to the original ode in order to avoid the stamp duty upon publications not exceeding a sheet. In those stanzas (17 to 19), which the author did not like, Napoleon is taken to task for having wanted a crown; if man wants to find in history a great person marred by neither 'guilty glory' nor 'despicable state', he must blushingly admit that there has been only one: Washington, the 'Cincinnatus of the West.'

Byron's hero-worship of Napoleon was rekindled when news of the latter's return to France on March 1, 1815 reached England, as witness his letter to Moore on March 27:

> If he can take France by himself, the devil's in't if he don't repulse the invaders, when backed by those celebrated sworders - those boys of the blade, the Imperial Guard, and the old and new army. It is impossible not to be dazzled and overwhelmed by his character and career. Nothing ever so disappointed me as his abdication, and nothing could have reconciled me to him but some such revival as his recent exploit; though no one could anticipate such a complete and brilliant renovation.

Byron wrote that letter from Seaham, where he and his bride had spent a couple of months after their honeymoon. About this time they left Seaham to take up residence in London, and Byron's biographers have enlarged upon the newly wedded Lord's marital relations, his debts, his meeting with Sir Walter Scott, his work on the Drury Lane Theatre Committee, etc.; but he also found time to attend debates in the House of Lords on Napoleon's escape from Elba and on the policy adopted by the British government at the Congress of Vienna.[5] He appears to have been under the influence of his friend John Cam Hobhouse, who believed that Napoleon was now willing to accept the role of a constitutional monarch, and who argued that surely it was for the French to choose their own head of state.

But the allied powers did not want Napoleon back; on June 18, 1815 the Battle of Waterloo was fought, and Paris was 'taken for a second time', as Byron has it in a letter to Moore dated 'July 7, 1815', in which he proceeds: 'Every hope of a republic is over, and we must go on under the old system.' Byron may here have in mind the constitutionalist and liberal decrees issued by Napoleon during the One Hundred Days; but what he means is rather that to him the decisive defeat of the French Empire amounted to the final abandonment of the ideas of the French Revolution, which was also Hobhouse's point of view. The Bourbons were restored! On April 19, 1814 that had caused an explosion on Byron's part in his journal. Even among the Tories there was widespread distrust of the Bourbons,[6] so the disgust expressed by Byron here is what we might expect: 'To be sure, I have long despised myself and man, but I never spat in the face of my species before'.

That the sixth Lord Byron attended debates in the House of Lords occasionally, was mentioned above. He had taken his seat in the House on March 13, 1809, two months after his coming of age. Then he had left England on his grand tour to return in July 1811, and on February 27, 1812 he had delivered his famous maiden speech on the 'framebreakers' or

'Luddites', followed on April 21, 1812 by a speech on Catholic emancipation and on June 1, 1813 by one on redress for Major Cartwright, who stood for parliamentary reform and had been dragged to court. As Malcolm Kelsall says in his *Byron's Politics*, (Harvester Press, 1987) p. 35:

> Byron's three speeches in the Lords concern classic Whig issues: conciliation of the grievances of the people, reform of the Constitution, the right to petition without hindrance for such reform.

Professor Kelsall demonstrates how Byron, in his political outlook, was steeped in Whig thought and attitudes, a position that had had its heyday in the 18th century when the great Whig families had run the country conceiving of themselves as defenders of freedom against that old monster, absolute monarchy. But by 1812 the Whigs had been out of office since 1783, and whereas their traditional attitude had made sympathy for the French Revolution possible among many Whigs in 1789, that position was becoming untenable under the impact of later developments in France. Thus in wishing Napoleon well, if only on the Continent, Byron was at variance with the majority of the Whigs, as he was in the case of the Cartwright petition. Naturally in both matters he was opposed to the Tories, whom he mostly despised and detested, Castlereagh in particular. The Tories were in office, and Byron was 'born for opposition' as he has it in *Don Juan*, XV, 22, adding in the next stanza:

> But then 'tis mostly on the weaker side:
> So that I verily believe if they
> Who now are basking in their full-blown pride,
> Were shaken down, and 'dogs had had their day,'
> Though at the first I might perchance deride
> Their tumble, I should turn the other way,
> And wax an ultra-royalist in loyalty,
> Because I hate even democratic royalty.

The relativism expressed here should not be taken to imply that Byron did not seriously have any convictions, as it would be erroneous to judge from his being 'greatly elated' by the compliments he received after his maiden speech that his performance on that occasion was a mere show for vanity's sake, though the young Lord undoubtedly loved to be praised for his oratory. In that speech the point is made clear that what some would call a 'mob' consists of hard-working people without whose exertions the country could not be rich and powerful; those people deserve our sympathy as much as foreign peoples suffering under a despotic rule, and if not treated in a civilized way the people could by neglect and calamity be driven to defy the Lords.[7] A few days later, on March 2, 1812, the *Morning Chronicle* published anonymously Byron's 'Ode to the Framers of the Frame Bill', another indication that he had taken to heart the plight of the Midland weavers who had in some cases smashed the modern machinery that would make less the demand for labour. In a letter to Lord Holland on February 25, 1812 Byron had expressed his fear that the government's bill would drive 'into actual rebellion' the 'miserable men', whose 'excesses may be condemned, but cannot be the subject of wonder'. In this letter he expresses himself much more guardedly than in the speech, not to mention the ode, and he even adds this P.S.:

> I am a little apprehensive that your Lordship will think me too lenient towards these men, & *half a framebreaker myself.*

Byron may have been an amateur in politics, as Georg Brandes and Erik Björkman assert;[8] in pleading the cause of the weavers of Nottinghamshire, where Newstead Abbey is situated, he certainly tried to behave as a responsible politician anxious to avoid a rebellion. He spoke as a Whig lord, but his passionate appeal on behalf of the working man of his day has become part of that man's heritage, and the gratitude of later generations of workers is testified by the visitors' book at the church of Hucknall Torkard, where the poet lies buried.[9]

Liberty, equality and fraternity were the three catchwords of the French Revolution. Byron cannot possibly be discussed without using the word 'liberty', whereas the two other words can be dispensed with. When pleading the cause of the framebreakers he spoke as the radical lord coming to the succour of distressed people; and the rebel heroes of his metrical tales are born leaders, clearly expressed in *The Corsair,* I, 187-90:

> Such hath it been - shall be - beneath the sun
> The many still must labour for the one!
> 'Tis Nature's doom - but let the wretch who toils
> Accuse not, hate not *him* who wears the spoils.

And when in *The Island* Byron reverted to his favourite hero for the last time, he described Fletcher Christian as 'of a higher order' (III, 139), i.e. once more inequality is stressed. When Byron wrote that, he had, it is true, also represented inequality as something instituted by man, namely in *Don Juan,* I, 194, where Donna Julia explains the very limited possibilities for a woman in a society dominated by the male sex; and in that poem we certainly come to realize that great and influential people are only human beings. Still, the word 'democracy' does not seem to make much sense in

115

connection with Byron; at any rate it would be much easier to make a case for Scott, who was always a Tory and detested the French Revolution, as being a democrat: the novelist who frequently depicted ordinary people as much nobler than the upper classes, as Bulwer-Lytton emphasized in his obituary of Scott in *The New Monthly Magazine*, 1832 (vol. 35, pp. 300-304).

Byron never forgot that he was a peer, and we have seen him assuming his hereditary obligation as champion of the oppressed; and though he cherished many radical views, he was not willing to lend his support to the views of such popular agitators as Hunt and Cobbett. That is obvious from his letter to Murray of February 21, 1820, where he comments, among other things, on Hobhouse's wish to stand for Westminster in the next Parliamentary election:

> I am out of all patience to see my friends sacrifice themselves for a pack of blackguards - who disgust one with their Cause - although I have always been a friend to and a Voter for reform. - If Hunt had addressed the language to me - which he did to Mr. H[obhouse] last election - I would not have descended to call out such a miscreant who won't fight but have passed my sword-stick through his body - like a dog's and then thrown myself on my Peers - who would I hope - have weighed the provocation; - at any rate - it would have been as public a Service as Walworth's chastisement of Wat. Tyler. - If we must have a tyrant - let him at least be a gentleman who has been bred to the business, and let us fall by the axe and not by the butcher's cleaver.

Byron ends the letter with this comparison of the English radical agitators and two cruel French revolutionaries:

> Lord George Gordon - and Wilkes - and Burdett - and Horne Tooke - were all men of education - and courteous deportment - so is Hobhouse - but as for these others - I am convinced - that Robespierre was a Child - and Marat a quaker in comparison of what they would be could they throttle their way to power.

John Murray in London undoubtedly agreed with Byron when he read this, as he must have been pleased to read the beginning of the letter, in which His Lordship regrets the death of George III in words very different from those in *The Vision of Judgment*, VIII:

> In the first year of Freedom's second dawn
> Died George the Third; although no tyrant, one
> Who shielded tyrants, till each sense withdrawn
> Left him nor mental nor external sun.

The year was 1820, and 'Freedom's second dawn' must be a reference to the revolutionary movements that had manifested themselves in Italy, Portugal and Spain. In his diary for January 13, 1821 Byron has the following comment on the renewal of revolutionary activities in the Europe of the Holy Alliance:

> Dined - news come - the *Powers* mean to war with the peoples. The intelligence seems positive - let it be so - they will be beaten in the end. The king-times are fast finishing. There will be blood shed like water, and tears like mist; but the peoples will conquer in the end. I shall not live to see it, but I foresee it.

The prospect does not fill him with enthusiasm, but the intelligence 'seems positive.' Eleven months earlier Byron had called himself a friend to reform; if the powers that be did not accept change they would have to perish: 'let it be so'.

About the same time Byron wrote his tragedy *Marino Faliero*, in which the scene is laid in the republic of Venice in a period of crisis. Marino Faliero, the Doge, feels that his honour is not being protected by the tribunal of the Forty, so he enters into an alliance with revolutionaries among the common people against his fellow aristocrats, which causes him split loyalties (I,ii, 579-588):

> At midnight, by the church Saints John and Paul,
> Where sleep my noble fathers, I repair -
> To what? to hold a council in the dark
> With common ruffians leagued to ruin states!
> And will not my great sires leap from the vault,
> Where lie two doges who preceded me,
> And pluck me down amongst them? Would they could!
> For I should rest in honour with the honour'd.

Marino Faliero hesitates to league with such people, but he does go to the meeting, where he promises the conspirators a better Venice (III,ii, 168-175):

> We will renew the times of Truth and Justice,
> Condensing in a fair free commonwealth
> Not rash equality but equal rights,
> Proportioned like the columns to the temple,
> Giving and taking strength reciprocal,
> And making firm the whole with grace and beauty,
> So that no part could be removed without
> Infringement of the general symmetry.

117

The Doge's ideas of a harmonious society are set forth beautifully, but the image clearly implies that complete equality is not thinkable. The Doge becomes the noble leader of the people against the powerful oligarchy, his own class; but the attempt proves unsuccessful, Marino Faliero is sentenced to death and executed, lamented by some as a friend to the people. Byron called his play 'an historical tragedy', i.e. the plan fails. If it had not done so, the Doge would have been a man after Byron's heart, a man like Sylla (i.e. Sulla), who was entrusted with power, finished the job, and then resigned, precisely what Napoleon had not done (see 'Ode to Napoleon Buonaparte', and Byron's diary for April 9, 1814). In his diary for November 23, 1813 Byron is concerned with Napoleon's dwindling power and complains that 'here we are, retrograding, to the dull, stupid old system, - balance of Europe - poising straws upon kings' noses, instead of wringing them off! Give me a republic, or a despotism of one, rather than the mixed government of one, two, three.' The best thing he could imagine for a man was to 'be the first man - not the Dictator - not the Sylla, but the Washington or the Aristides - the leader in talent and truth.' Byron adds that he himself will 'never be any thing'; still, this entry was certainly written by somebody who knew his own worth. But Byron was also proud of being a peer, which is hard to reconcile with his hostility to the monarchy, for it was King Charles I who in 1643 had created Sir John Byron Baron Byron of Rochdale in the County of Lancaster.[10]

Probably Byron had the impression that in a republic people are automatically more free than in a monarchy. At any rate 'freedom' and 'liberty' must be key-words in any discussion of him. One of his most beautiful poems, *The Prisoner of Chillon*, is a monologue by a man who had become so accustomed to the dungeon that he regained his 'freedom with a sigh.' Byron advocated political as well as national liberty, as witness his support for the Italian Carbonari against the Austrians and his death in Missolonghi as a participant in the Greek War of Independence. From boyhood he had loathed control or repression of himself, personal liberty was dear to him, and in *Don Juan*, IX, 24-25 he expresses the idea that man may become the slave of anybody:

And I will war, at least in words (and - should
My chance so happen - deeds) with all who war
With Thought; - and of Thought's foes by far most rude,
Tyrants and Sycophants have been and are.
I know not who may conquer: if I could
Have such a prescience, it should be no bar
To this my plain, sworn, downright detestation
Of every despotism in every nation.

It is not that I adulate the people:
Without *me*, there are Demagogues enough,
And Infidels, to pull down every steeple
And set up in their stead some proper stuff.
Whether they may sow Scepticism to reap Hell,
As is the Christian dogma rather rough,
I do not know; - I wish men to be free
As much from mobs as kings - from you as me.

The first of those two stanzas deals with liberty of thought, the aspect of Byron that looms particularly large in Brandes' representation of him. That aspect is very well illustrated by the wide scope of *Don Juan*, which shows, for instance, a shipwreck as both ludicrous and moving, and which so often challenges our conventional ideas and stock responses.

Vivian de Sola Pinto, who delivered the 21st Byron Foundation Lecture in Nottingham University in 1944, chose as his subject 'Byron and Liberty.' He traces changes in the semantic meaning of the word, and praises Byron as one of those who protested against the complacency with which liberty was regarded and as a 'writer who gave a new meaning and a new urgency to the word Liberty.' When Pinto delivered his lecture, it was clear that the 'great Fascist plot' against freedom had failed, and in the great struggle freedom had had as its ally the poet who coined 'the two great phrases which have heartened the democracies in their struggle against Nazi, - Fascist tyranny, "blood, sweat and tears" and "united nations"'.[11]

There are many other aspects of Byron's life and work that deserve our attention, but his concern with liberty is one of his greatest legacies to posterity. Pinto's lecture clearly acknowledges that. Byron's concept of freedom bears the mark of Rousseau (Juan is a natural man, as Haidée is a natural woman), and his political ideals were shaped by Whig attitudes and by what he had read about antiquity and America, rather than by the French Revolution. But the political developments he reacted to were those of the decades following 1789; in an age of tranquility his poetry 'would have lost half its motive power.'[12] The renewed revolutionary activities of the 1820s were seen by him as a second dawn of liberty, and to contemporaries and to the following generations Byron's poetry was the expression of the spirit of liberty that had been awakened by the French Revolution. Thus the young Icelander Grimur Thomsen asserts in his thesis *Om Lord Byron*, p. 233 (Copenhagen, 1845) that only Byron's poetry made the French Romantics aware of 'the central principle of the Revolution, the liberty of thought,' and in Russia the poet Ryleyev went to the scaffold in 1826 with a volume of Byron under his shirt.[13] So the interesting question may not be what Byron thought of the French Revolution, but what his readers have thought of him.

Notes

1. L.A. Marchand, *Byron*, Vol. I (London, 1957), p. 34; Michael Foot, *The Politics of Paradise: A Vindication of Byron* (London, 1988), p. 90.
2. *Childe Harold, The Corsair* and 'Ode to Napoleon' are here quoted from Lord Byron, *The Complete Poetical Works*, ed. by Jerome J. McGann, Vols. II-III (Oxford, 1980-81); *Don Juan* from the 'Variorum Edition', Vols II-III ed. by Steffan and Pratt (University of Texas Press, 1957); other poems from E.H. Coleridge's edition of Byron's *Poetry*, I-VII (London, 1903-1905).
3. Paul Holzhausen, *Bonaparte, Byron und die Briten* (Frankfurt a.M., 1904) is particularly valuable for the enormous material amassed by the author. A much more scholarly work is Gerhard Eggert, *Lord Byron und Napoleon*, Palaestra 186 (Leipzig, 1933). A shorter modern study, which brings in some new material, is James Hogg, 'Byron's Vacillating Attitude Towards Napoleon' in Erwin A. Stürzl & James Hogg, (eds.), *Byron: Poetry and Politics*, Salzburger Studien zur Anglistik und Amerikanistik 13 (Salzburg, 1981). That volume, the proceedings of the Seventh International Byron Symposium, Salzburg 1980, has in many ways influenced the present paper.
4. Letters and diaries are quoted from *Byron's Letters and Journals*, Vols. 1-12, ed. by Leslie A. Marchand (London, 1973-1982).
5. L.A. Marchand, *Byron*, Vol. II (London, 1957), p. 533.
6. Holzhausen, op.cit., pp. 136 and 165.
7. Similarly, in his reply to Southey's attack on the 'Satanic school' Byron sees the French Revolution (here clearly the 'revolution proper') as provoked by the oppression of the government (*The Works of Lord Byron. Letters and Journals*, ed. by R. E. Prothero, Vol. VI (London, 1904), pp. 387-389.
8. Georg Brandes in his *Naturalismen i England, Hovedstrømninger i det nittende Aarhundredes Litteratur*, IV (Copenhagen, 1924), p. 129; Erik Björkman in 'Lord Byron och politiken', *Ord och Bild*, Vol. 26 (Stockholm, 1917), pp. 289-290.
9. Malcolm Kelsall, 'Byron, a personal appreciation' in *Byron 1788-1824* (catalogue of the British Council Byron exhibition, 1988). Evidence of Byron's impact on the Chartists is discussed by Foot, op.cit., pp. 387-390.
10. *The Story of the Abbey*, Newstead Abbey Publications No. 1 (Corporation of Nottingham, 1945).
11. V. de Sola Pinto, *Byron and Liberty*, Byron Foundation Lecture 1944 (The University of Nottingham, 1944). For the two phrases, Pinto refers us to *The Age of Bronze*, XIV, 621 and to *Childe Harold*, III, 35.
12. Edward Dowden, *The French Revolution and English Literature* (London, 1897), p. 158 .
13. Eóin MacWhite, 'Thomas Moore and Nineteenth Century Russian Literature' in *Escape*, Vol. 3 (Groningen, 1971), pp. 211-213 .

Two books to which the present writer feels indebted, but which have not been mentioned in the notes, are Crane Brinton, *The Political Ideas of the English Romanticists* (Oxford U.P., 1926) and Carl Woodring, *Politics in English Romantic Poetry* (Harvard U.P., 1970).

Shelley's Demogorgon:
The Spirit of Revolution Internalized

Karsten Klejs Engelberg

Ever since his own day, Shelley has been perceived by critics as a revolutionary poet. The literary establishment of his time saw him as a threat to the existing social order; *Queen Mab* became the Chartist's Bible in the 1840s, and Karl Marx's daughter, Eleanor, gave a lecture on Shelley's socialism in 1885.[1] Twentieth-century politicians have peppered their speeches and writings with Shelley quotations, and Paul Foot's recent *Red Shelley*[2] presented the poet as an indispensable inspiration for everyone working for radical changes in society.[3]

In his early youth, Shelley himself was active in support of various radical causes. He went to Dublin to demonstrate his sympathy for the movement for Catholic emancipation,[4] and for a while he worked as a fund raiser for William Madocks's dam project in North Wales.[5] These activities, though, invariably led to frustrations for Shelley. He left Dublin, deeply disappointed by a tepid and, as he saw it, uncomprehending response to his ideas, and attempted to spread his message to the Irish by various highly unconventional, but equally ineffective, means.[6] His sojourn in Wales ended very abruptly in the curious shooting incident at Tan-yr-allt which, whatever the truth of the matter may have been, certainly signalled Shelley's difficulties in working for the people he wished to help.[7] He never really meddled in practical politics after that. So, although Shelley's radical sympathies remained constant, he had great difficulties deciding on means and methods.

The French Revolution was all history to him, albeit quite recent history. The France he knew was that of the post-revolutionary, Napoleonic era. Unlike his older contemporaries, notably Wordsworth, he had not lived through the painful trauma of seeing the ideals of liberty and equality produce, in a matter of just a few years, an excessively repressive regime. He never had to face the temptation of rejecting out of hand the ideals of the French Revolution as dangerously frivolous and scurry back to the safety of a firm social order. True, he experienced disappointment in Dublin and Wales, but it was of a kind that sharpened the beliefs that had inspired his involvement, not something that induced him to change his social and political outlook completely. In fact, his experience produced his particular brand of thinking, which was unusual in Britain in the aftermath of the French Revolution, combining as it did an abhorrence for the political and social manifestations of the French Revolution with an unruffled adherence to the basic moral principles that inspired it. His particular concept of revolution - a word, incidentally, that he hardly ever used in his writings - rejected the need for violence and for sudden abrupt social upheaval while emphasizing the need for constant change and for a constant personal awareness of the moral principles that must be reflected in all social relations: justice, equality, and love. This concept found its fullest manifestation in *Prometheus Unbound*, but as we shall see, this presupposed a gradual distancing himself from the world of practical politics, coupled with a step-by-step distillation from the events of this world of the principles which each and every individual must fight to maintain. In this sense, the French Revolution was both a regrettable historical event of the past and an ongoing process of constant moral awareness, an event that has never been completed.

In the days of his early youth, Shelley was never afraid of provoking the Establishment in writings of obvious and direct criticism. He got himself expelled from Oxford for arguing the case of *The Necessity of Atheism*, and as late as 1819, his fellow liberal Leigh Hunt refused to publish *The Masque of Anarchy*, Shelley's direct and indignant comment on the Peterloo Massacre. This period is full of Shelley's outraged criticism of political repression and violence, and the tone of the texts is invariably harsh, stirring, and uncompromising, full of the elements of traditional revolutionary rhetoric. *Queen Mab* abounds in examples:[8]

> Let the axe
> Strike at the root, the poison-tree will fall;
> And where its venomed exhalations spread
> Ruin, and death, and woe, where millions lay
> Quenching the serpent's famine, and their bones
> Bleaching unburied in the putrid blast,
> A garden shall arise, in loveliness
> Surpassing fallen Eden. (IV, 82-89)

The spectrum of Shelley's attacks was broad: the Established Church:

> Falsehood demands but gold to pay the pangs
> Of outraged conscience; for the slavish priest
> Sets no great value on his hireling faith:
> A little passing pomp, some servile souls,
> Whom cowardice itself might safely chain,
> Or the spare mite of avarice could bribe
> To deck the triumph of their languid zeal,
> Can make him minister to tyranny. (V, 197-204)

kings:

> The King, the wearer of a gilded chain
> That binds his soul to abjectness, the fool
> Whom courtiers nickname monarch, whilst a slave
> Even to the basest appetites - that man
> Heeds not the shriek of penury; he smiles
> At the deep curses which the destitute
> Mutter in secret, ... (III, 30-36)

and politicians:

> And statesmen boast
> Of wealth! The wordy eloquence, that lives
> After the ruin of their hearts, can gild
> The bitter poison of a nation's woe,
> Can turn the worship of the servile mob
> To their corrupt and glaring idol, Fame,
> From Virtue, trampled by its iron tread,
> Although its dazzling pedestal be raised
> Amid the horrors of a limb-strewn field,
> With desolated dwellings smoking round. (V, 93-102)

In 1821 Shelley denounced the poem in a letter to the editor of *The Examiner* as 'crude and immature', claiming himself worried that the poem 'is better fitted to injure than to serve the sacred cause of freedom'.[9] Nevertheless, poems of harsh revolutionary rhetoric kept appearing from his pen all through his career.

But Shelley's distrust of direct, sudden and sweeping action gradually changed his concept of the true nature of revolution. His most extended poetical comment on the French Revolution, *The Revolt of Islam*, represents an important step in this development. Full of stirring, uncompromising attacks on authority, even endorsing the use of violence against a repressive regime, the poem ends in the failure of the revolution.[10] But it is the failure of the revolution only in specific, political terms. Far from being dejected by their failure, the two leaders of the revolution, Laon and Cythna, leave their earthly life on a triumphant journey to the realm of everlasting love. The survival of the revolutionary spirit was of much greater importance than any temporary change in practical political conditions.

A sonnet, 'Feelings of a Republican on the Fall of Bonaparte', published in 1816, clarifies this suspicion of the importance of specific political events. The opening strikes the tone of the revolutionary mode:

> I hated thee, fallen tyrant!

but rather than developing into a celebration of the demise of a tyrant, the poem ends in a realization that Napoleon was a mere product of history and that his downfall is no ultimate victory. The true enemies of freedom and justice remain and cannot be defeated just through political actions:

> I know
> Too late, since thou and France are in the dust,
> That virtue owns a more eternal foe
> Than Force or Fraud: old Custom, legal Crime,
> And bloody Faith the foulest birth of Time. (ll. 10-14)

Shelley's apparent denial of the relative importance of the here and now has earned him the reputation of being a head-in-the-clouds idealist.[11] But he was himself aware of the dangers inherent in the suggestion that life here and now is of importance only as a manifestation of some larger principles. The poet in *Alastor*, which was published with the Bonaparte poem discussed above, meets a sorry end for the very reason that his all-consuming search for ultimate truths makes him unfit to lead an ordinary life among people. The poet dies alone, no nearer to the fulfilment of his dream of discovering these ultimate truths than he was at the outset.

If we return for a moment to Shelley's Irish campaign, its failure is a clear example of this opposition between revolutionary ideals and revolutionary practice. He addressed political activists, eager for immediate social and legal reforms, but he was not prepared to endorse any violent changes:[12]

> Many circumstances, I will own, may excuse what is called rebellion, but no circumstances can ever make it good for your cause, and however honourable to your feelings, it will reflect no credit on your judgment. (p. 47)

Instead, he advocated a purely intellectual approach.

> Be calm, mild, deliberate, patient; recollect that you can in no measure more effectually forward the cause of reform than by employing your leisure time in reasoning or the cultivation of your minds. (p. 46)

This was not an approach that his readers were prepared patiently to adopt. It offered no hope of the immediate changes that they felt were urgently required. As we have seen, Shelley repeatedly adopted the tone of violent revolutionary rhetoric; yet he was never fully satisfied that such an approach would produce other than a simple rearrangement of existing conditions. A genuine revolution must go deeper than that and yet not degenerate into an idealistic, intellectual quest, like that of the poet in *Alastor*, wholly disconnected from man's physical existence.

With the advantage of hindsight, Shelley could dismiss the French Revolution as a clear example of the first type of revolution which failed because it degenerated into a simple power struggle:

> The French Revolution, although undertaken with the best intentions, ended ill for the people, because violence was employed. (p. 47)

In another essay, inspired by the Irish question, 'An Association of Philanthropists', Shelley offered a fuller account of the failure of the French Revolution. He accepts that it was inspired by 'the literary labours of the Encyclopedists', but the advocacy of liberty, justice, and equality by writers such as D'Alembert, Boulanger, and Condorcet can in no way be said to have occasioned the 'bloodshed, vice, and slavery' (p. 67) which came to mark the French Revolution. The prolonged enslavement of the French people had rendered them totally unfit to understand fully the nature of this promised freedom.

> Since the French were furthest removed by the sophistications of political institutions from the genuine condition of human beings, they must have been most unfit for that happy state of equal law which proceeds from consummated civilization and which demands habits of the strictest virtue before its introduction. (p. 67)

Shelley repeated his account of the failure of the French Revolution in 'A Philosophical View of Reform' and in the preface to *The Revolt of Islam* in which he describes 'liberal-minded, forbearing, and independent' citizens as 'the consequence of the habits of a state of society to be produced by resolute perseverance and indefatigable hope, and long-suffering and long-believing courage, and the systematic efforts of generations of men of intellect and virtue'. The French Revolution had not happened as a result of this. 'Thus, many of the most ardent and tender-hearted of the worshippers of public good have been morally ruined by what a partial glimpse of the events they deplored appeared to show as the melancholy desolation of all their cherished hopes'.[13]

Shelley retained his interest in political and social affairs, but at various times he found them difficult to handle in practice. In 1815, he complained to Thomas Jefferson Hogg:

> In considering the political events of the day I endeavour to divest my mind of temporary sensations, to consider them as already historical. This is difficult. Spite of ourselves the human beings which surround us infect us with their opinion: so much as to forbid us to be dispassionate observers of the question arising out of the events of the age.[14]

And three years earlier, he had expressed his intense dislike of the study of history:

> I am determined to apply myself to a study that is hateful and disgusting to my very soul, but which is above all studies necessary for him who would be listened to as a mender of antiquated abuses. - I mean that record of crimes and miseries - History.[15]

Although the world of practical politics became ever more distasteful to him, he remained a keen observer of the political scene in Europe and was ready to express his high hopes for the success of any attempt to overthrow repressive regimes. He kept writing verse in the revolutionary mode of political agitation, but *Prometheus Unbound* became his finest, most comprehensive statement on the nature of true revolt, a statement which allowed Shelley to reconcile the contradictions of his own beliefs in liberty and justice with his dislike of practical politics and his own disappointments in this sphere. In doing so, he salvaged the high ideals of the French Revolution from the 'gloom and misanthropy' which 'have become the characteristics of the age in which we live, the solace of a disappointment that unconsciously finds relief only in the wilful exaggeration of its own despair'.[16] He removed the revolutionary spirit from the realm of history and politics and made it a permanent, necessary, and deeply individual state of mind.

The drama opens in the Caucasus, with Prometheus tied to a rock. He is as adamantly uncompromising as ever in his hatred of Jupiter. We recognize the tone and imagery of the traditional revolutionary mode when Prometheus welcomes

The wingless, crawling hours, one among whom
- As some Priest hales the reluctant victim -
Shall drag thee, cruel King, to kiss the blood
From these pale feet ...   (I, 48-51)

But then he claims

I speak in grief,
Not exultation, for I hate no more,
As then ere misery made me wise.   (I, 56-58)

The Earth is distressed at Prometheus's apparent loss of the will to oppose Jupiter.

Misery, Oh misery to me,
That Jove at length should vanquish thee.
Wail, howl aloud, Land and Sea,
The Earth's rent heart shall answer ye.   (I, 306-309)

But Prometheus is not prepared to submit.

Let others flatter Crime, where it sits throned
In brief Omnipotence ...   (I, 400-401)

A band of furies appears from Jupiter to torment Prometheus. They revel in their own evil, and Prometheus asks

Can aught exult in its deformity?
Second Fury. The beauty of delight makes lovers glad,
Gazing on one another: so are we.
As from the rose which the pale priestess kneels
To gather for her festal crown of flowers
The aëreal crimson falls, flushing her cheek,
So from our victim's destined agony
The shade which is our form invests us round,
Else we are shapeless as our mother Night. (I, 465-472)

Evil feeds on evil, and a fury asks Prometheus if he thinks that he can escape their evil in the form of 'dread thought beneath thy brain, / And foul desire round thine astonished heart' (I, 488-489) to which Prometheus answers

Why, ye are thus now;
Yet am I king over myself, and rule
The torturing and conflicting throngs within, (I, 491-493)

Before they depart, one of the furies paints a bleak picture of the imperfections of human life:

> In each human heart terror survives
> The ravin it has gorged: the loftiest fear
> All that they would disdain to think were true:
> Hypocricy and custom make their minds
> The fanes of many a worship, now outworn.
> They dare not devise good for man's estate,
> And yet they know not that they do not dare.
> The good want power, but to sweep barren tears.
> The powerful goodness want: worse need for them.
> The wise want love; and those who love want wisdom;
> And all best things are thus confused to ill.
> Many are strong and rich, and would be just,
> But live among their suffering fellow-men
> As if none felt: they know not what they do. (I, 618-631)

She cannot comprehend Prometheus's proud answer to this:

> Thy words are like a cloud of wingéd snakes;
> And yet I pity those they torture not. (I, 632-633)

Prometheus accepts human imperfection as inherent in the human condition. And when the fury has left, Prometheus wails

> Ah woe!
> Ah Woe! Alas! pain, pain ever, for ever!
> I close my tearless eyes, but see more clear
> Thy works within my woe-illuminéd mind,
> Thou subtle tyrant! (I, 634-638)

A group of spirits now appear to speak to Prometheus's despair. They remind him that Man's hope for a better future 'begins and ends in thee' (I, 707). This hope is bred by the spirit of love, and the words of the spirits rekindle Prometheus's love for Asia, whom he has neglected ever since he took up the cause of fighting for man's freedom. Asia has been consigned by this neglect to exile in a cold and distant valley, but the rebirth of Prometheus's love for her has transformed the scene of her exile so that it is now

> ... invested with fair flowers and herbs,
> And haunted by sweet airs and sounds, which flow
> Among the woods and waters, from the aether
> Of her transforming presence, which would fade

If it were mingled not with thine. (I, 829-833)

Asia is stirred by this change and goes in search of Prometheus. On her way she visits the Cave of Demogorgon. She is accompanied by Panthea who wonders

> I see a mighty darkness
> Filling the seat of power, and rays of gloom
> Dart round, as light from the meridian sun.
> - Ungazed upon and shapeless; neither limb,
> Nor form, nor outline; yet we feel it is
> A living Spirit. (II, iv, 2-7)

This is Demogorgon, whom Asia asks to explain the origins of all things good and evil. She wants a name from Demogorgon, but he will not supply it. He simply echoes Asia's own thoughts until she asks, 'Who is the master of the slave?' (II, iv, 114), to which he responds:

> If the abysm
> Could vomit forth its secrets. ... But a voice
> Is wanting, the deep truth is imageless;
> For what would it avail to bid thee gaze
> On the revolving world? What to bid speak
> Fate, Time, Occasion, Chance, and Change? To these
> All things are subject but eternal Love. (II, iv, 114-120)

Asia realises that Demogorgon is a power within herself which reinforces her own thoughts and desires:

> So much I asked before, and my heart gave
> The response thou hast given; and of such truths
> Each to itself must be the oracle. (II, iv, 121-123)

She is immediately taken away by the Immortal Hours: 'Some look behind, as fiends pursued them there, /... / Others, with burning eyes, lean forth, and drink / With eager lips the wind of their own speed, / As if the thing they loved fled on before' (II, iv, 133-137). But the Spirit of the Hour pauses on the brink between night and day, and Asia voices her newfound insight:

> ... all love is sweet,
> Given or returned. Common as light is love,
> And its familiar voice wearies not ever.
> Like the wide heaven, the all-sustaining air,
> It makes the reptile equal to the God:
> They who inspire it most are fortunate,

As I am now; but those who feel it most
Are happier still, after long sufferings,
As I shall soon become. (II, v, 39-47)

At the opening of Act III, Jupiter is discovered sitting on his throne.
He rejoices in his near-supreme power:

... henceforth I am omnipotent.
All else had been subdued to me; alone
The soul of man, like unextinguished fire,
Yet burns towards heaven with fierce reproach ... (III, i, 3-6)

But Demogorgon, released by Asia's realization of the power of love,
appears and dethrones Jupiter. Prometheus is released and can rejoice in
reports of the changes which the unleashed power of love has worked on
earth:

All things had put their evil nature off ... (III, iv, 77)

And behold, thrones were kingless, and men walked
One with the other even as spirits do,
None fawned, none trampled; hate, disdain, or fear,
Self-love or self-contempt, on human brows
No more inscribed, as o'er the gate of hell,
'All hope abandon ye who enter here;' (III, iv, 131-136)

Had the poem ended here, it would have been little more than a modified
repetition of the agitator's revolutionary dream: a paradise established on
earth through the overthrow of tyranny. But two concepts have played a
major role in most of the quotations given above: the indispensable
reciprocity of all human emotion without which, ultimately, all human life
ceases, and the constant changes of life on earth. And Act III ends on a
note of recognition that although feasible, the paradisal state of freedom and
justice is inherently volatile.

The loathsome mask has fallen, the man remains
Sceptreless, free, uncircumscribed, but man
Equal, unclassed, tribeless, and nationless,
Exempt from awe, worship, degree, the king
Over himself; just, gentle, wise: but man
Passionless? - no, yet free from guilt or pain,
Which were, for his will made or suffered them,
Nor yet exempt, though ruling them like slaves,
From chance, and death, and mutability,
The clogs of that which else might oversoar

The loftiest star of unascended heaven,
Pinnacled dim in the intense inane. (III, iv, 193-204)

Shelley added a truly remarkable fourth act to his drama. It portrays in a giddy whirl of images the amazing powers which have been released in the Universe by Prometheus's victory. But the act also serves as a vehicle for Demogorgon's final warning. He appears at the very end of Act IV to join in the celebration of the success of the revolution. The tone of his closing speech is optimistic, but there is no mistaking the warning that tyranny may well re-establish itself.

Gentleness, Virtue, Wisdom, and Endurance,
These are the seals of that most firm assurance
    Which bars the pit over Destruction's strength;
And if, with infirm hand, Eternity,
Mother of many acts and hours, should free
    The serpent that would clasp her with his length;
These are the spells by which to reassume
An empire o'er the disentangled doom.
To suffer woes which Hope thinks infinite;
To forgive wrongs darker than death or night;
    To defy Power, which seems omnipotent;
To love, and bear; to hope till Hope creates
From its own wreck the thing it contemplates;
    Neither to change, nor falter, nor repent;
This, like thy glory, Titan, is to be
Good, great and joyous, beautiful and free;
This is alone Life, Joy, Empire, and Victory. (IV, 562-578)

Demogorgon was the instrument of freedom, but he is no power independent of individual man. He can only respond, as he did to Asia, to the desires and wishes of individual man. Just like Prometheus, individual man may grow proud and set in his ways, even if those ways are pain and slavery. He may believe, as did Prometheus, that his fierce resistance to tyranny is justified by some vision of the common weal. But Prometheus's victory was secured not by this belief, but by a recognition of the fellowship of man, the power of love. He could not win his victory on his own; only when his recognition of his love for Asia silenced his condescending disdain for Jupiter did he win his victory.

Prometheus is a god who can show man the way. But man must actively seek that way, the way of love. And man remains the slave of 'chance, and death, and mutability'. Escape from this state of bondage is possible only through the constant reaffirmation of the benign qualities of Demogorgon, a constant pouring forth of hope, forgiveness, and love.

Change itself is an inescapable condition of human life. Social and political revolutions are in themselves mere products of this condition. The true revolution lies in constant self-improvement, but even this can degenerate into a static principle, as in the case of Prometheus at the beginning of the play. Man must accept mutablility and change as inescapable, but he must not be content merely to serve as their slave. Nor must he turn his back on them and try to ignore their existence. That is the fallacy of the poet in *Alastor*. He must feel the power of love within him through all changes and make sure that he acts upon this power in the temporal human world, through all its changes. But unlike his previous revolutionary poems, *Prometheus Unbound* is not just a hopeful celebration of the ultimate victory of revolution and a stirring denunciation of all tyranny. Demogorgon is the true revolutionary spirit, embodying simultaneously both the failure and success of all change. Success can only be ensured through constant personal moral awareness, because ultimately 'The deep truth is imageless'.

Notes

1. A modern edition of this is Edward & Eleanor Marx Aveling, *Shelley's Socialism* (Manchester: Preger, 1947).
2. Paul Foot, *Red Shelley* (London: Sidgwick & Jackson, 1980).
3. For full accounts of Shelley's critical reputation and reprints of critical texts, see e.g. Newman Ivey White (ed.), *The Unextinguished Hearth: Shelley and His Contemporary Critics* (Durham, North Carolina: Duke University Press, 1938); Sylvia Norman, *Flight of the Skylark: The Development of Shelley's Reputation* (London: Max Reinhardt & Norman, Oklahoma: University of Oklahoma Press, 1954); Timothy Webb, *Shelley: A Voice Not Understood* (Manchester: Manchester University Press, 1977), 1-32; Karsten Klejs Engelberg, *The Making of the Shelley Myth: An Annotated Bibliography of Criticism of Percy Bysshe Shelley, 1822-1860* (London: Mansell & Westport, Conneticut: Meckler, 1988).
4. See Newman Ivey White, *Shelley*, 2 volumes (New York: Alfred A. Knopf, 1940), I, pp. 206-221.
5. For details of Shelley's involvement, see White, *Shelley*, I, pp. 255-258, 265-269, 280-285, and Richard Holmes, *Shelley: The Pursuit* (London etc.: Oxford University Press, 1970).
6. See Holmes, pp. 148-149.
7. See Holmes, pp. 187-188, 190-197.
8. All quotations from Shelley's poems follow the text in Percy Bysshe Shelley, *Political Works*, ed. Thomas Hutchinson, rev. by G.M. Matthews (London etc.: Oxford University Press, 1970). Line references for each quotation will be given in the text, and the edition will be referred to in subsequent notes as *PW*.
9. *PW*, p. 838.

10. For a detailed account of the parallels, see Kenneth Neill Cameron, 'The Political Symbolism of Prometheus Unbound' in R.B. Woodings (ed.), *Shelley: Modern Judgments* (London: Macmillan, 1969), pp. 102-129. In January 1812, Shelley was working on plans for a novel entitled *Hubert Cauvin*. See Frederick L. Jones (ed.), *The Letters of Percy Bysshe Shelley*, 2 vols. (Oxford University Press, 1964), I, pp. 218, 223, 229. Shelley intended 'to exhibit the cause of the failure of the French Revolution' (*Letters*, I, p. 218), but he seems never to have completed this plan.
11. See note 3 above.
12. All quotations from Shelley's prose follow David Lee Clark (ed.), *Shelley's Prose: or, the Trumpet of a Prophecy* (Albuquerque: The University of New Mexico Press, 1954). Page references appear in the text at the end of each quotation.
13. *PW*, p. 33.
14. *Letters*, I, p. 430.
15. *Letters*, I, p. 340.
16. *PW*, p. 33.

Suggested further reading

Cameron, Kenneth Neill, *Shelley: the Golden Years*. Cambridge, Mass.: Harvard University Press, 1974

Cameron, Kenneth Neill, *The Young Shelley: Genesis of a Radical*. New York & London: Macmillan, 1951.

Hogle, Jerrold E., *Shelley's Process: Radical Transference and the Development of His Major Works*. London etc.: Oxford University Press, 1988.

White, Harry, 'Relative Means and Ends in Shelley's Social-Political Thought'. *SEL: Studies in English Literature, 1500-1900*, 22 (1982), 613-631.

Carlyle and Dickens on the French Revolution
A Stylistic Study

Knud Sørensen

1. The French Revolution

Thomas Carlyle published his monumental work, *The French Revolution*, in 1837, after a prolonged and laborious process of composition. We can follow this process step by step in his correspondence.[1] He had read copiously on the subject, not least books lent to him by John Stuart Mill, and in 1834 had reached a point where he found further reading useless: 'My grand task, as you already know, is the *French Revolution*; which, alas, perplexes me much. More *Books* on it, I find, are but a repetition of those before read; I learn nothing or almost nothing further by Books ...'[2] But despite difficulties and '*Bedenklichkeiten* of all kinds'[3] he slogged away at his task.

Then, in early 1835, disaster struck. Carlyle had lent Mill the first volume of his manuscript, which was 'by him too carelessly, *sent up the chimney*, as kindling for fires!'[4] Carlyle had no copy of the manuscript, but with unquenchable energy he threw himself into rewriting it, a task that he referred to as 'the unspeakablest load'.[5] In a letter to his mother he even endeavoured to persuade himself and her that something good might come of it: '... I had determined that there must be a finger of Providence in it; that it meant simply I was to write the thing over again *truer* than it was'[6] - though elsewhere he complains that he has '"the Bastille to take" a *second* time'.[7] But he got through his tough struggle, finishing the book in early 1837.

As already mentioned, Carlyle voices misgivings about his work, and he predicts that it will be a queer book (though perhaps more readable than

The Dolphin 19
©Aarhus University Press 1990

Sartor Resartus).[8] Posterity has confirmed this verdict. As for the queerness, it may be worth looking in some detail at the manner in which Carlyle goes about his task.

One feels that it is Carlyle's prime endeavour to carry his reader with him through a narrative that is characterized by a high degree of drama and immediacy. His style is emphatic and vociferous. He frequently apostrophizes his reader:

Reader, fancy not, in thy languid way, that Insurrection is easy. (2.13.6)[9]

or his characters:

Yes, persist, O infatuated Sansculottes of France! (2.8.2)
Thou laggard sonorous Beervat, with the loud voice and timber-head, is it time now to palter? (2.13.6)

He is fond of rhetorical questions, as appears from the preceding quotation and those that follow:

Is not Sentimentalism twin-sister to Cant, if not one and the same with it? (1.2.7)
Is there a man's heart that hears it without a thrill? (2.13.3)

and he spices his account with dramatic interruptions:

Sleek Pache, the Swiss Schoolmaster, he that sat frugal in his Alley, the wonder of neighbours, has got lately - whither thinks the Reader? To be Minister of War! (3.15.2)

Most of the narrative is couched in the dramatic present, tending to imply 'the contemporaneity of events'.[10] But sometimes it is varied by abrupt tense-shifts:

Suddenly, however, one of these men steps forward. He had on a blue frock-coat; ... 'Which way?' cried he to the Brigands: 'Show it me, then.' They open the folding gate ... (3.14.4)

A more extended quotation will show some of the other devices that Carlyle typically resorts to in order to convey his special tone; the passage given below describes the activities in July 1792 of the Duke of Brunswick, one of the commanders of the allied Austrian and German army whose aim was to crush the French Revolution:

135

Mark contrariwise how, in these very hours, dated the 25th, Brunswick 'shakes himself, *s'ébranle*,' in Coblentz; and takes the road! Shakes himself indeed; one spoken word becomes such a shaking. Successive, simultaneous *dirl* of thirty-thousand muskets shouldered; prance and jingle of ten thousand horsemen, fanfaronading Emigrants in the van; drum, kettledrum; noise of weeping, swearing; and the immeasurable lumbering clank of baggage-wagons and camp-kettles that groan into motion: all this is Brunswick shaking himself; not without all this does the one man march, 'covering a space of forty miles.' Still less without his Manifesto, dated, as we say, the 25th; a State-Paper worthy of attention! (2.13.3)

Here, after the first couple of lines the present tense is replaced by a nominal style that dispenses with most finite verbs; this amounts to a listing of features that together contribute to conjuring up the scene. The Carlylean penchant for litotes is exemplified twice in this passage, and one further notes the word *dirl*, characteristic of Carlylese (see below) as well as the presence of two quotations from a State Paper. It is Carlyle's practice to intersperse his account with such quotations to strengthen its ring of authenticity, and he often introduces snippets of French. Sometimes a French quotation precedes its English translation, sometimes it is the other way round:

Stupid Peter Baille almost made an epigram, though unconsciously, ... when he wrote: '*Tout va bien ici, le pain manque*, All goes well here, food is not to be had.' (2.12.8)

Fiery Max Isnard ... is for declaring 'that we hold Ministers responsible; and that by responsibility we mean death, *nous entendons la mort*.' (2.12.7)

In many passages the dramatic character of Carlyle's account is reinforced through his use of heavily punctuated periods consisting of short members; this kind of sentence organization spells abruptness and speed, at the same time suggesting a segmentation characteristic of spoken language:[11]

Speeches are spoken; a judgment is held, a doom proclaimed, audible in bull-voice, towards the four winds. (2.11.2)

Lafayette flings down his Commission; appears in civic pepper-and-salt frock; and cannot be flattered back again; not in less than three days; and by unheard-of entreaty ... (2.11.1)

The kind of punctuation employed in such passages forces the reader to attach full and equal importance to each of the items; compare 'Gone are the Jacobins; into invisibility; in a storm of laughter and howls.' (3.20.4).

136

A favourite syntactic pattern with Carlyle is the one in which what in an unemphatic formulation would be the predicative appears in extraposition in a nominal construction, the fronted item thus receiving strong emphasis; there is an exclamatory ring to this construction: 'A singular thing this Camp of Jalès' (2.8.2); 'An anomalous class of mortals these poor Hired Killers!' (2.9.2); 'An intrepid adamantine man, this Bouillé' (2.9.6).

There are various other devices that Carlyle resorts to in order to secure the reader's attention, among them chiastic word-order: 'Their Formalism is great; great also is their Egoism' (3.16.4); the foregrounding of predicatives and objects: 'Aristocrats almost all our Officers necessarily are' (2.9.2); 'Him, in a night-foray at Maubeuge, the Austrians took alive ...' (3.18.6); and a zeugmatic construction that sometimes accommodates irony: 'Reason ... escorted by wind-music, red nightcaps, and the madness of the world.' (3.18.4). A note of irony may also be detected where emphatic repetition occurs:

> The Sedan Municipals obey.
>   The Sedan Municipals obey; but the Soldiers of the Lafayette Army? The soldiers of the Lafayette Army have ... a kind of dim feeling that they themselves are Sansculottes in buff belts ... (2.13.8)

Further striking features are the numerous instances of alliteration: 'great Journalism blows and blusters' (2.10.2); 'A tragical combustion, long smoking and smouldering' (2.12.3); 'wise wigs wag, taking what counsel they can' (2.12.5); 'whole Armies and Assemblages will sing it ... with hearts defiant of Death, Despot and Devil' (2.13.2). There are also many rhyming tags: 'National Assembly Commissioners ... strive in all wise ways to smooth and soothe' (2.9.6); 'The heads of men are saddened and maddened' (2.11.1); 'La Vendée ... has not ceased grumbling and rumbling' (2.12.6); 'sitting there ... quivering and shivering' (2.13.6); and occasional examples of assonance, sometimes made a vehicle for punning: 'Louis Capet was only called Inviolable by a figure of rhetoric; but at bottom was perfectly violable, triable' (3.15.4). Carlyle's message is further brought home through a generous use of triplets: 'The multitude ... pounces on them [arms]; struggling, dashing, clutching' (1.5.6); 'A most blinkard, bespectacled, logic-chopping generation' (2.8.2).

Carlyle has a pronounced penchant for punning. Some of his puns are in rather poor taste, reminding one of the Danish writer Grundtvig's feebler efforts. Here are a few specimens:

much flowing matter there is ... about Right, Nature, Benevolence, Progress; which flowing matter, whether 'it is pantheistic', or is pot-theistic, only the greener mind ... need examine. (2.10.2)

Breathless messengers, fugitive Swiss, denunciatory Patriots, trepidation; finally tripudiation! (2.13.8)

How astonishing that in a time of Revolt and abrogation of all Law but Cannon Law, there should be such Unlawfulness? (3.15.2)

In the preceding pages we have looked at some of the syntactic and stylistic features that contribute to making Carlyle's a *marked* style. When we turn to his vocabulary, we shall also find him deviating from the normal, unmarked language of his day.

Above, we noted the word *dirl*, a Scottish or northern dialectal form meaning 'thrill, vibration'; there occur similar northern forms like *ingate* (2.12.2, = 'entrance') and *outgate* (2.13.6, = 'exit'). Verbs beginning with the prefix *be-* are great favourites with Carlyle: 'They are ... bedinnered, begifted' (2.12.10); 'Not ten days hence Patriot Brissot, beshouted this day by the Patriot Galleries, shall find himself begroaned by them' (2.13.3).

There occur many peculiar and rare words. Thus we come across words like *eleutheromania* 'mad zeal for freedom' (1.3.4), *quotity* 'number' (1.4.2), and *goadster* 'a driver who uses a goad' (2.10.7). Instead of the normal form *eyesore* Carlyle prefers *eye-sorrow*: 'Papal Aristocrats and Patriot Brigands are still an eye-sorrow to each other' (2.13.3), and he uses *body-politic* to coin an analogous form: 'An instantaneous change of the whole body-politic, the soul-politic being all changed' (3.15.1). Other Carlylean coinages are *astucity* 'astuteness' (3.14.13) and *fremescent* 'murmuring' (2.13.7), and he is bold enough to create his own translation of a French word: 'It is the first of the *Noyades*, what we may call *Drownages*' (3.18.3). Adjectival, more or less unorthodox, compounds are extremely numerous, for instance *querulous-indignant* (2.9.3), *feeble-petulant* (2.12.1) *real-imaginary* (2.12.3), *implacable-impotent* (2.12.8), and *tearful-boastful* (3.14.1), to mention but a few.

Another favourite with Carlyle is the conversion of nouns into verbs, a process that produces examples like the following: 'Serene Highnesses, who sit there protocolling and manifestoing' (2.13.3); 'Neither do men now *monsieur* and *sir* one another' (3.14.1): 'With hard wrestling, with artillerying and *ça-ira*-ing, it shall be done' (3.18.6).

Finally, we may note a pronounced tendency for Carlyle to employ abstract terms in concrete senses; several instances of his usage are so idiosyncratic as not to have been recorded by the OED. Here are some examples: 'Mutiny continues firing' (2.9.6); 'bereaved down-beaten

Patriotism murmurs' (2.9.6); 'Brilliancies, of valour and of wit stroll here observant' (2.12.1); 'half-drunk Rascality offers him a bottle' (2.12.12).[12]

So far, no mention has been made of one stylistic peculiarity that suggests something about Carlyle's attitude to the historical drama that he portrays. This is a characteristic use of the pronouns *we*, *us*, and *our*; for instance:

> On the night of that same twenty-eighth of August ... Dumouriez assembles a Council of War ... He spreads out the map of this forlorn war-district; Prussians here, Austrians there; triumphant both, with broad highway, and little hinderance, all the way to Paris: we scattered, helpless, here and here: what to advise? (3.14.3)

> And now behold Marat meets us; for he lagged in this Suppliant Procession of ours ... (3.16.9)

In such passages the narrator temporarily identifies with the revolutionaries, most often with what he terms *Patriotism*; and this narrative empathy is sometimes extended to those imprisoned by the revolutionaries: 'Suspicious Municipality snatches from us all implements' (3.19.5) and even to the instigators of the King's abortive attempt at flight: 'Crack, crack, we go ...cessant, through the slumbering City.' (2.11.3), but not to the Jacobin extremists. The use of *we* in these and similar passages reflects the narrator's changing perspective, in its turn evidence of his endeavour to arrive at balance and fairness in his account of the terrible events.

The Carlylean philosophy underlying the account of the entire period from 1774 to 1795 is not systematically expounded, but crops up in various passages. It is strongly tinged with mysticism. The entire universe 'is but an infinite Complex of Forces ... the All of Things is an infinite conjugation of the verb *To Do* ... human things wholly are in continual movement, and action and reaction ... How often must we say, and yet not rightly lay to heart: The seed that is sown, it will spring!' (2.10.1). But very few people are able to see this. Those few individuals are people gifted with a kind of superior intuition (those whom he was later to term 'heroes'); for Carlyle is a believer in intuition and instinct rather than in logic and objectivity; instinct is truer than thought.

What characterizes the world through the ages - continual movement - also characterizes the events he describes; the French Revolution is an exemplification of the universe, and it is described as 'a single integrated movement' having a cosmic significance.[13] But there is the difference that the revolutionary period is characterized by the speed with which events take place. There is, further, a movement from sham to reality; à propos of May 4, 1789 he writes: 'This day, sentence of death is pronounced on Shams;

judgment of resuscitation, were it but afar off, is pronounced on Realities' (1.4.4) - the facts of history thus embodying a moral lesson.

But has the Revolution fostered no 'heroes'? Yes, one man, Mirabeau: 'A man not with *logic-spectacles*; but with an *eye!*' (1.4.4) - a man who might have prevented many gross excesses had he not died prematurely (2.10.6). The long pre-Revolutionary period of despotism and injustice, during which the French population were destined to live 'Untaught, uncomforted, unfed; to pine stagnantly in thick obscuration, in squalid destitution and obstruction' (1.1.2), was bound to lead to violent upheaval. With the removal of shams, the age of miracles has come back:

> Behold the World-Phoenix, in fire-consummation and fire-creation: wide are her fanning wings; loud is her death-melody, of battle-thunders and falling towns; skyward lashes the funeral flame, enveloping all things: it is the Death-Birth of a World! (1.6.1)

But alas, with Mirabeau dead, this birth can lead but to chaos and massacre, and ultimately to the rise of a Bonaparte.

Carlyle is an earnest seeker after the truth as he sees it, and despite his distrust of objectivity it is obvious that he studied the available historical sources diligently. It has been estimated that he drew on at least 83 sources, mainly memoirs, reminiscences, hastily written histories, letters, and diaries, from which he selected and transformed numerous passages that were carefully arranged so as to form a vast word-picture.[14] Sometimes he complains about the meagreness of his sources: 'So vague are all these; *Moniteur, Histoire Parlementaire* are as good as silent: garrulous History, as is too usual, will say nothing where you most wish her to speak!' (2.13.2). His account is an odd mixture of descriptions based on contemporary sources, often incorporating extended quotations from them, alternating with his own comments, frequently of a moral character: 'O poor mortals, how ye make this Earth bitter for each other; this fearful and wonderful Life fearful and horrible; and Satan has his place in all hearts!' (1.5.5). Another recurrent feature is prophetic and warning statements: 'Poor M. de Gouvion is ... a man shiftless, perturbed: who will one day commit suicide.' (1.7.4); 'Let that rock-fortress, Tyranny's stronghold, which they name *Bastille*, or *Building*, as if there were no other building, - look to its guns!' (1.4.3).

But the vast panorama conjured up is really just a fraction of the whole, there being limits to what the historian can cope with; but perhaps he can attempt a 'flame-picture':

But the hundredth part of the things that were done, and the thousandth part of the things that were projected and decreed to be done, would tire the tongue of History. ...

On the whole, is it not, O Reader, one of the strangest Flame-Pictures that ever painted itself; flaming off there, on its ground of Guillotine-black? And the nightly Theatres are Twenty-three; and the *Salons de danse* are Sixty; full of mere *Égalité, Fraternité* and *Carmagnole*. And Section Committee-rooms are Forty-eight; redolent of tobacco and brandy: vigorous with twenty-pence a day, coercing the Suspect. And the Houses of Arrest are Twelve, for Paris alone; crowded and even crammed ... (3.18.7)

2. *A Tale of Two Cities*

A Tale of Two Cities was printed serially in *All the Year Round* from April to November 1859 and was published in book form in November of that year. It appears from the Preface that Dickens got the idea for the plot from Wilkie Collins's play *The Frozen Deep*, and he was probably also inspired by Bulwer-Lytton's novel *Zanoni* (1845).[15] But for the Paris scene before and during the Revolution he drew on Carlyle:

It has been one of my hopes to add something to the popular and picturesque means of understanding that terrible time, though no one can hope to add anything to the philosophy of Mr. CARLYLE's wonderful book.

This was a book that Dickens was thoroughly familiar with; as he says in a letter to Forster: ' ... reading that wonderful book the *French Revolution* for the 500th time ...'[16] He was a great admirer of Carlyle and regarded him as his mentor, and when publication of *A Tale of Two Cities* had begun, Dickens was happy to inform Forster: 'A note I have had from Carlyle about it has given me especial pleasure.'[17]

In a number of respects Dickens's indebtedness to Carlyle is obvious. The two books cover roughly the same time, and both make a point of emphasizing how the intolerable conditions of the pre-Revolutionary period were bound to lead to an explosion. Dickens was no theorist or philosopher, and it is perhaps doubtful to what extent he had absorbed that part of Carlyle's philosophy which regarded the Revolution as an exemplification of the universe; the following passage appears, however, to convey a similar idea:[18]

Château and hut, stone face and dangling figure, the red stain on the stone floor, and the pure water in the village well - thousands of acres of land - a whole province of France - all France itself - lay under the night sky, concentrated into a faint hair-breadth line. So does a whole world, with all its greatnesses and littlenesses, lie in a twinkling star. (2.16.168)

Carlyle provides portraits of a great number of prominent revolutionaries, which Dickens does not. His characters are fictitious, with one exception: he refers to the capture of 'old Foulon, who told the famished people that they might eat grass' (2.22.212). For this point he is indebted to *The French Revolution*, 1.5.9. Some of the names that appear in *A Tale of Two Cities* were no doubt suggested by Carlyle's work: *Tellson*'s Bank, which figures so prominently in the novel, was adapted from *Thelusson*'s Bank, where Necker was once a clerk (*The French Revolution*, 1.2.5), and the local tax-collector, M. *Gabelle*, owes his name to the term for the salt tax imposed before the Revolution, *la gabelle*.[19] One further notes a semantic loan inspired by Carlyle: 'Sheep was a cant word of the time for a spy, under the gaolers' (3.8.282). This use of the word is not recorded by the OED, but Dickens must have taken his cue from the following passage in *The French Revolution*: 'He has his *moutons*, detestable traitor jackals, who report and bear witness' (3.19.5).

A stylistic comparison between the two works reveals some interesting similarities. In the first place Carlyle's empathetic *we*, employed when the narrator wishes to identify with the people he describes, has a curious parallel in Dickens. In the description of the flight from Paris, the fugitives express fears of pursuit, but one of them reassures the others: 'So far, we are not pursued.' (3.13.339). This statement is followed by a one-page account of their further progress, an account whose form proclaims it as third-person narrative, but in which *we* and *us* have been retained: 'Houses in twos and threes pass by us ... Sometimes, we strike into the skirting mud ...', a highly unconventional device that enables Dickens to heighten the sense of danger through empathy with the fugitives.

Another stylistic feature of the novel is the foregrounded predicative construction that was noted as a characteristic of Carlyle's style: 'A wonderful corner for echoes, ... that corner where the Doctor lived' (2.21.200). There are other similarities, for instance the tendency for both writers to indulge in nominal style and to make prophetic statements of an ominous character. Here is an example of the latter, where wine symbolizes blood: 'The time was to come, when that wine too would be spilled on the street-stones, and when the stain of it would be red upon many there.' (1.5.28). Besides, *A Tale of Two Cities* has examples of sound devices like rhyme ('staring and blaring', 2.2.58; 'driving and riving', 2.5.84) and alliteration ('rush and roar', 2.6.97; 'no pause, no pity, no peace', 3.4.259). But these devices are common everywhere in Dickens and were not necessarily inspired by Carlyle.

But apart from the inspiration that he received from Carlyle, Dickens left his own personal stamp on his novel. Not that it can be termed a typical Dickensian novel. In the first place it is a historical novel (for which only *Barnaby Rudge* provides a partial parallel), and this is brought home through the repeated use of expressions like *in those days* and *at that time*. In the second place it is comparatively short, and this has had the consequence that the author relies much less on dialogue than in most of his other works; Dickens himself referred to this fact by speaking of the need for 'incessant condensation'.[20] This again means that there is much less humour and raciness in *A Tale of Two Cities* than in his other novels; almost the only attempt at humorous characterization is represented by Jerry Cruncher, the body-snatcher.

Despite these differences a number of characteristically Dickensian features are noteworthy. For one thing, there is his tendency to see everything in black-and-white terms: the good characters are mostly very noble while the bad characters are thoroughly bad. This is something of an artistic drawback. Then there is Dickens's well-known tendency to overwrite; the sombre aspects of his topic lead him to describe 'Hungry Saint Antoine' (a Parisian suburb, stronghold of the Revolution) in the following manner:

> ... the children had ancient faces and grave voices; and upon them, and upon the grown faces, and ploughed into every furrow of age and coming up afresh, was the sign, Hunger. It was prevalent everywhere. Hunger was pushed out of the tall houses, in the wretched clothing that hung upon poles and lines; Hunger was patched into them with straw and rag and wood and paper; Hunger was repeated in every fragment of the small modicum of firewood that the man sawed off; Hunger stared down from the smokeless chimneys ... (1.5.28f)

Similar heavy emphases occur elsewhere.

But there are also parts of the book that impress one by their stylistic sophistication, for instance the descriptions of the Mail travelling from London to Dover (1.2) and of Monseigneur's journey to his château (2.8). In another passage Dickens demonstrates the virtuosity with which he is capable of conveying a precise impression of a court interrogation through his handling of free indirect speech:

> Had he ever been a spy himself? No, he scorned the base insinuation. What did he live upon? His property. Where was his property? He didn't precisely remember where it was. What was it? No business of anybody's. Had he inherited it? Yes, he had. From whom? Distant relation. Very distant? Rather. Ever been in prison? Certainly not. Never in a debtors' prison? Didn't see what that had to do with it. Never in a debtors' prison? - Come, once again. Never? Yes. ... (2.3.63)

This, in condensed form, produces a vivid idea of the actual words used by the interlocutors.

As to symbolism, it has already been mentioned that wine symbolizes blood - sometimes in rather a crude manner: 'Six tumbrils carry the day's wine to La Guillotine.' (3.15.353). Another recurring symbol is knitting. The revolutionary women and particularly Mme Defarge are described as knitting all the time, Mme Defarge knitting a record of doomed enemies (2.1.164); elsewhere the knitting is associated with 'the steadfastness of Fate' (2.7.106), and in front of the Guillotine we find the terrible *tricoteuses* 'seated in chairs, as in a garden of public diversion ..., busily knitting' (3.15.355).

The novel is dominated by the cognate themes of Revolution and Resurrection. Revolution is a process of death and rebirth, and the related theme of Resurrection is given a Christian interpretation in connection with the self-sacrifice of Sydney Carton, whose execution is preceded by a biblical quotation: 'I am the Resurrection and the Life, saith the Lord' (3.15.357), and who at the foot of the scaffold makes an imaginary speech, in the course of which he says: 'I see the evil of this time and of the previous time of which this is the natural birth, gradually making expiation for itself and wearing out.' So the novel ends on a comparatively optimistic note after the characters have lived through 'the best of times' and 'the worst of times'. Perhaps this reflects Dickens's own domestic problems that confronted him while he was writing the book. He separated from his wife in 1859 and may have believed that he was 'recalled to life' by the young actress Ellen Ternan with whom he then formed a union.[21]

The title of the novel implies a stark contrast between revolutionary Paris and peaceful London. However, it is also relevant to call attention to the very first chapter of the book, in which it is pointed out that the time of the Revolution resembles 'the present period', and that in both countries, at the end of the eighteenth century, 'it was clearer than crystal to the lords of the State preserves of loaves and fishes, that things in general were settled for ever' (1.1.1). Thus there is complacency to be found in both countries, as well as a serious misconception as to the causes of the Revolution:

> It was too much the way of Monseigneur [as a representative of the French aristocracy] under his reverses as a refugee, and it was too much the way of native British orthodoxy, to talk of this terrible Revolution as if it were the one only harvest ever known under the skies that had not been sown ... (2.24.226)

The message is clear enough: what happened in France might well happen in England. Carlyle's work is meant as a warning, and so is Dickens's.

Notes

1. *Letters of Thomas Carlyle 1826-1836*. Edited by Charles Eliot Norton in two volumes, London and New York 1888.
2. Letter of August 15, 1834, to his brother John, Norton II, p. 210.
3. Ibid.
4. Letter of October 21, 1835, to Henry Inglis, Norton II, p. 379. Carlyle reports the disaster to several correspondents, but this is the report that most clearly accounts for the fate of the manuscript.
5. Norton II, p. 347.
6. Letter of March 25, 1835, Norton II, p. 302.
7. Norton II, p. 314.
8. His biographer J.A. Froude comments as follows on Carlyle's style: 'The humour of it came from his mother. The form was his father's common mode of speech, and had been adopted by himself for its brevity and emphasis. He was aware of its singularity and feared that it might be mistaken for affectation, but it was a natural growth, with this merit among others, that it is the clearest of styles.' (*Thomas Carlyle. A History of His Life in London 1834-1881*, two volumes, London 1902; vol. I, p. 42).
9. Quotations are from *The French Revolution. A History by Thomas Carlyle*, London and New York 1904. 2.13.6 = Part II, Book XIII, Chapter VI, etc.
10. Chris R. Vanden Bossche: 'Prophetic Closure and Disclosing Narrative: *The French Revolution* and *A Tale of Two Cities*', in DICKENS STUDIES ANNUAL, vol. 12, New York 1983, p. 212.
11. Cf. *The Norton Anthology of English Literature*, revised edition, New York 1968, vol. 2, p. 746: '... Carlyle has contrived to get the sound of his own spoken voice into his writings.'
12. A detailed examination of word-formation in Carlyle is Otto Schmeding: *Über Wortbildung bei Carlyle*, Halle a.S. 1900.
13. John Holloway: *The Victorian Sage*, London 1953, p. 61.
14. C.F. Harrold: 'Carlyle's General Method in *The French Revolution*', PMLA XLIII, 1928, pp. 1150-1169.
15. Earle Davis: *The Flint and the Flame. The Artistry of Charles Dickens*, University of Missouri Press, Columbia 1963, p. 248.
16. John Forster: *The Life of Charles Dickens*, I-II, Everyman's Library 1980, vol. II, p. 57.
17. Forster, vol. II, p. 281.
18. Quotations are from *The Oxford Illustrated Dickens* (Oxford: Oxford University Press, 1949, reprinted 1987), with indications of Book, Chapter, and page.
19. Earle Davis, p. 248.
20. Forster, vol. II, p. 281.
21. Cf. Jack Lindsay: *Charles Dickens. A Biographical and Critical Study*, London 1950; Morton D. Zabel: *Craft and Character*, New York 1957, pp. 59-60.

Notes on Contributors

John Dussinger (University of Illinois, Urbana-Champaign), professor of English. He has written numerous essays on eighteenth-century literature. Among his publications are *The Discourse of the Mind in Eighteenth-Century Fiction* (1974) and *In the Pride of the Moment: Encounters in Jane Austen's World* (1990).

Karsten Klejs Engelberg (Copenhagen International School) is a graduate of the University of Copenhagen and has a D. Phil. from the University of Oxford. He is the author of *The Making of the Shelley Myth* (London, 1988), and editor of *The Romantic Heritage* (Publications of the Department of English, Copenhagen 1983).

Anders Iversen (University of Aarhus) teaches English and American history and literature. He has written articles on twentieth-century writers and edited *The Dolphin* No. 16, *Something to Believe In: Writer Responses to the Spanish Civil War* (1988).

Ib Johansen (University of Aarhus) teaches literature in the English Department. Among his publications are books and articles on William Blake, on fantastic literature and science fiction. He is editor of an anthology of *Fantastic Tales* (1983) and co-editor of *The Dolphin* No. 11: *Inventing the Future*. He has also written a collection of poems in English, *The Mystery Garden and Other Poems* (1979).

The Dolphin 19
©Aarhus University Press 1990

Mel Leiman (State University of New York at Binghamton), professor of Economics. He has written on the history of economic thought, socialist theory, and comparative politics. His forthcoming study of *The Political Economy of Racism* will be published by Pluto Press.

Jørgen Erik Nielsen (University of Copenhagen), reader in the Department of English. His dissertation (1976) is on *Den samtidige engelske litteratur og Danmark 1800-1840* (Denmark 1800-1840 and Contemporary English Literature).

Per Serritslev Petersen (University of Aarhus) has written essays on Jane Austen, D.H. Lawrence, Jack London, romanticism and primitivism, and on literary theory. He is co-editor of an anthology of contemporary British drama, *British Drama in the Eighties* (1986).

Knud Sørensen (University of Aarhus), professor of English. Among his many books are *Charles Dickens: Linguistic Innovator* (1985) and *English Past and Present* (1988).